The Death Penalty

OTHER BOOKS OF RELATED INTEREST

The Death Penalty

Hayley R. Mitchell, *Book Editor*

Contemporary Issues
Companion

Greenhaven Press, Inc., San Diego, CA

Every effort has been made to trace the owners of copyrighted material. The articles in this volume may have been edited for content, length, and/or reading level. The titles have been changed to enhance the editorial purpose. Those interested in locating the original source will find the complete citation on the first page of each article.

Library of Congress Cataloging-in-Publication Data

The death penalty / Hayley R. Mitchell, book editor.
        p.   cm. — (Contemporary issues companion)
    Includes bibliographical references and index.
    ISBN 0-7377-0457-8 (pbk. : alk. paper) —
ISBN 0-7377-0458-6 (lib. bdg. : alk. paper)
    1. Capital punishment—United States. I. Mitchell, Hayley R.,
1968–   . II. Series.

HV8699.U5 D634 2001
364.66'0973—dc21   00-029405
                                                                          CIP

©2001 by Greenhaven Press, Inc.
P.O. Box 289009, San Diego, CA 92198-9009

Printed in the U.S.A.

CONTENTS

FOREWORD

In the news, on the streets, and in neighborhoods, individuals are confronted with a variety of social problems. Such problems may affect people directly: A young woman may struggle with depression, suspect a friend of having bulimia, or watch a loved one battle cancer. And even the issues that do not directly affect her private life—such as religious cults, domestic violence, or legalized gambling—still impact the larger society in which she lives. Discovering and analyzing the complexities of issues that encompass communal and societal realms as well as the world of personal experience is a valuable educational goal in the modern world.

Effectively addressing social problems requires familiarity with a constantly changing stream of data. Becoming well informed about today's controversies is an intricate process that often involves reading myriad primary and secondary sources, analyzing political debates, weighing various experts' opinions—even listening to firsthand accounts of those directly affected by the issue. For students and general observers, this can be a daunting task because of the sheer volume of information available in books, periodicals, on the evening news, and on the Internet. Researching the consequences of legalized gambling, for example, might entail sifting through congressional testimony on gambling's societal effects, examining private studies on Indian gaming, perusing numerous websites devoted to Internet betting, and reading essays written by lottery winners as well as interviews with recovering compulsive gamblers. Obtaining valuable information can be time-consuming—since it often requires researchers to pore over numerous documents and commentaries before discovering a source relevant to their particular investigation.

Greenhaven's Contemporary Issues Companion series seeks to assist this process of research by providing readers with useful and pertinent information about today's complex issues. Each volume in this anthology series focuses on a topic of current interest, presenting informative and thought-provoking selections written from a wide variety of viewpoints. The readings selected by the editors include such diverse sources as personal accounts and case studies, pertinent factual and statistical articles, and relevant commentaries and overviews. This diversity of sources and views, found in every Contemporary Issues Companion, offers readers a broad perspective in one convenient volume.

In addition, each title in the Contemporary Issues Companion series is designed especially for young adults. The selections included in every volume are chosen for their accessibility and are expertly edited in consideration of both the reading and comprehension levels

7

of the audience. The structure of the anthologies also enhances accessibility. An introductory essay places each issue in context and provides helpful facts such as historical background or current statistics and legislation that pertain to the topic. The chapters that follow organize the material and focus on specific aspects of the book's topic. Every essay is introduced by a brief summary of its main points and biographical information about the author. These summaries aid in comprehension and can also serve to direct readers to material of immediate interest and need. Finally, a comprehensive index allows readers to efficiently scan and locate content.

The Contemporary Issues Companion series is an ideal launching point for research on a particular topic. Each anthology in the series is composed of readings taken from an extensive gamut of resources, including periodicals, newspapers, books, government documents, the publications of private and public organizations, and Internet websites. In these volumes, readers will find factual support suitable for use in reports, debates, speeches, and research papers. The anthologies also facilitate further research, featuring a book and periodical bibliography and a list of organizations to contact for additional information.

A perfect resource for both students and the general reader, Greenhaven's Contemporary Issues Companion series is sure to be a valued source of current, readable information on social problems that interest young adults. It is the editors' hope that readers will find the Contemporary Issues Companion series useful as a starting point to formulate their own opinions about and answers to the complex issues of the present day.

INTRODUCTION

The Universal Declaration of Human Rights issued by the United Nations on December 10, 1948, states in part that "no one shall be subjected to torture or to cruel, inhuman, or degrading punishment." While the Declaration of Human Rights does not specifically forbid the death penalty, since the declaration's inception, numerous nations have adopted the view that the death penalty constitutes cruel and inhuman punishment. Therefore, over the last fifty years, abolition of the death penalty has increased significantly worldwide. As of 1995, fifty-four countries had completely abolished capital punishment, and fifteen nations had abolished it for all but war crimes. Ninety-seven countries retained the death penalty, but of these, twenty-seven had not carried out any executions for ten years. On average, two countries abolish the death penalty per year. The United States, however, still practices capital punishment.

Despite America's current retention of the death penalty, the Supreme Court's findings on the subject have not always remained constant. On July 29, 1972, for example, the Supreme Court found in *Furman v. Georgia* that the death penalty was unconstitutional as practiced because its arbitrary application violated the Eighth Amendment, which forbids cruel and unusual punishment. The *Furman* ruling involved three separate cases in which African American defendants were sentenced to death for the murder or rape of white victims. In reviewing these three cases, the Court ruled that in each one, the death penalty had been unfairly and arbitrarily applied. The justices pointed to statistical evidence showing that if the defendants in these cases had been white, they would have been more likely to receive lesser sentences. In considering the cases, Justice William Douglas wrote:

> A law that stated that anyone making more than fifty thousand dollars would be exempt from the death penalty would plainly fall, as would a law that in terms said that blacks, those who never went beyond the fifth grade in school, or those who made less than three thousand dollars a year, or those who were unpopular or unstable should be the only people executed. A law, which in the overall view reaches that result in practice has no more sanctity than a law which in terms provides the same.

Ruling thus that the death penalty was imposed too arbitrarily to justify its constitutionality, the Court placed a moratorium on capital sentences while various lower courts worked to rectify the procedural problems throughout the system that had contributed to the unconstitutional application of the death penalty. The lives of more than six hundred prisoners were spared during this time. Meanwhile, thirty-five state legislatures developed new capital punishment laws that were designed to satisfy the Court's requirements for fairness and consistency.

The Supreme Court passed judgment on one of these new statutes on July 2, 1976, in the case of Troy Gregg, a man sentenced to death for armed robbery and murder under a post-*Furman* law in Georgia. In *Gregg v. Georgia*, the Court found that the imposition of the death penalty for murder did not necessarily constitute cruel and unusual punishment under the Eighth Amendment in all circumstances. Writing in support of the Court's ruling, Justice Potter Stewart commented that "the most marked indication of society's endorsement of the death penalty for murder is the legislative response to *Furman.*" Public opinion polls in 1976 echoed this observation, revealing that 66 percent of Americans were in favor of death penalty sentences for those convicted of murder. After this ruling, death penalty sentencing and executions resumed in Georgia and many other states, although some retained state bans on capital punishment.

Despite the Court's ruling in *Gregg v. Georgia*, death penalty opponents have continued to focus on the administration of the death penalty, claiming that its application remains arbitrary, unfair, and racist. These critics maintain that in some states, the disparity between the number of blacks and whites on death row is rapidly increasing. According to *Philadelphia Magazine*, for example, in 1995 the ratio of black to white prisoners on Pennsylvania's death row was seventy-four to forty-six; African Americans represented only 9 percent of Pennsylvania's population, but 61 percent of the death row population was black. Such disproportionate ratios can be found throughout the nation, opponents argue: Although blacks comprise a smaller portion of the population than whites, they consistently outnumber whites on death row.

Those concerned about racial inequalities in death penalty sentencing fear that lawmakers are more concerned with swift punishment than true justice in their efforts to expand the number of crimes for which capital punishment can be imposed. The more crimes punishable by death, they warn, the more minorities will end up on death row. Another source of concern for opponents of capital punishment is the elimination of funding for death penalty resource centers, which provide legal representation for defendants who cannot afford legal counsel. Without access to these centers, critics insist, minority defendants often receive inadequate counsel by court-appointed defense attorneys who are overworked, ill-prepared, and underpaid. These critics maintain that since poor defendants—who are often racial minorities—typically have substandard legal representation, they are far more likely than rich defendants to receive the death penalty. "The way the system treats people is skewed according to economic class," asserts Noelle Hanrahan of Equal Justice USA.

While death penalty opponents work to prove that capital punishment is still applied in an uneven and arbitrary manner, proponents of the death penalty claim that there is no solid evidence of racial bias in post-*Furman* judgments. Many argue that any apparent disparity can be attributed to higher criminal rates among blacks and other minorities. For instance, John J. DiIulio Jr., a professor of politics and public affairs at Princeton University, contends that

> of those persons under sentence of death in 1993, about 58 percent were white. This is actually much higher than the proportion of all murderers who are white. Historically, black homicide rates have never been less than five times white homicide rates, and in many years since the 1950s have been more than 10 times higher.

Although DiIulio and other supporters of capital punishment do not feel that racial bias exists within the system, they do believe that the American justice system is in need of reform because only a small percentage of convicted murderers are ever actually executed. They maintain that the debate over racial bias in capital sentencing has contributed to a harmful delay in justice, one which the average U.S. citizen does not support. Death penalty dissenters, DiIulio suggests, should respect the fact that most Americans value the death penalty: "Every major opinion survey of the last decade shows that large majorities of Americans—whites, blacks, young and old alike—support the execution of murderers."

The debate over whether racial bias plays a role in death penalty sentencing is just one of the many controversies concerning capital punishment. Because the disagreements over the death penalty are unlikely to be resolved any time soon, it is important to gain an understanding of the issues surrounding the topic. The authors included in *Death Penalty: Contemporary Issues Companion* provide a wide array of opinions, statistics, and insights on both sides of this controversy, illuminating the persistent debate over the justness of the ultimate punishment.

CHAPTER 1

THE DEATH PENALTY: AN OVERVIEW

THE DEATH PENALTY AND THE CAPITAL TRIAL

Mark Costanzo and Lawrence T. White

Mark Costanzo teaches psychology at Claremont McKenna College and Claremont Graduate School in Claremont, California. Lawrence T. White teaches at Beloit College in Beloit, Wisconsin. In the following article, Costanzo and White present a brief history of the death penalty in the United States. They also examine recent trends in the administration of the death penalty, such as the reduction in the number and types of crimes punishable by death, the development of more humane forms of execution, the attempt to impose fair and rational death sentences, and the removal of executions from public view. The authors discuss the American system of capital jurisprudence and explain the financial cost of the death penalty and its accompanying procedures.

The value of the death penalty is passionately debated in homes, schools, courtrooms, and the halls of Congress. The key arguments that fuel our continuing national debate over capital punishment could be heard in the highest court in the land. Arguing against the death penalty in an eloquent dissent in 1994, Justice Harry Blackmun declared, "From this day forward, I no longer shall tinker with the machinery of death." He described the execution process in graphic terms: "Intravenous tubes attached to his arms will carry the instrument of death, a toxic fluid designed specifically for the purpose of killing human beings . . . no longer a defendant, . . . but a man, strapped to a gurney and seconds away from extinction." Justice Antonin Scalia countered Blackmun's statements by describing the brutal rape and murder of an 11-year-old girl and declaring "How enviable a quiet death by lethal injection compared with that!" Blackmun further argued that "the death penalty remains fraught with arbitrariness, discrimination, caprice, and mistake," that "race continues to play a major role in determining who shall live and who shall die," and that "the death penalty, as currently administered, is unconstitutional." Scalia responded that "If the people conclude that more brutal deaths may be deterred by capital punishment; indeed, if they merely conclude that justice requires such brutal deaths

Excerpted from "An Overview of the Death Penalty and Capital Trials: History, Current Status, Legal Procedures, and Cost," by Mark Costanzo and Lawrence T. White, *Journal of Social Issues*, vol. 50, no. 2, Summer 1994. Reprinted with permission from Blackwell Publishers.

to be avenged . . . the Court's Eighth Amendment jurisprudence should not prevent them.". . .

The Death Penalty in the United States

Nearly four centuries have passed since the first documented execution on American soil took place in 1608. Early colonial laws concerning capital punishment were borrowed from British law. Under British law, more than 50 crimes were designated as capital offenses including vagrancy, heresy, witchcraft, rape, murder, and treason. Eventually, the American colonies developed their own lists of capital crimes. These lists varied widely. For example, Puritan-influenced Massachusetts Bay Colony listed statutory rape, rebellion, adultery, buggery, idolatry, witchcraft, bestiality, man stealing, and blasphemy as capital crimes. In contrast, Quaker-influenced South Jersey declined to adopt capital punishment in its original charter. Many early lists of capital offenses included acts that threatened the prevailing social-economic order. North Carolina's list, for example, included circulating seditious literature among slaves, inciting slaves to insurrection, stealing slaves, and harboring slaves for the purpose of setting them free. Similarly, Virginia listed only five capital crimes for whites, but 70 for blacks.

Progress of the movement to abolish the death penalty has been slow and erratic. In 1794, Pennsylvania restricted use of the death penalty to first-degree murder and in 1834 became the first state to ban public executions. A few states went even further. Michigan eliminated capital punishment for all crimes except treason in 1846. Rhode Island and Wisconsin became the first two states to eliminate capital punishment for all crimes in 1852 and 1853, respectively. However, most states that experimented with abolition later reinstated the death penalty (e.g., Colorado, New Mexico, Ohio, and Oregon). As of 1994, 37 states and the federal government have statutes authorizing capital punishment. (Alaska, Hawaii, Iowa, Maine, Massachusetts, Michigan, Minnesota, New York, North Dakota, Rhode Island, Vermont, West Virginia, and Wisconsin do not have the death penalty.)

Throughout U.S. history, the number of death sentences and executions has always been small when compared with the number of murders. Individuals convicted of murder rarely are executed. The rate of executions reached a record high in 1938, when there were 2.01 executions per 100 homicides in states with the death penalty. It is estimated that less than 10% of capital homicides—those the legal system considers to be the worst possible murders—result in executions. The annual number of executions was highest during the 1930s, peaking in 1935 when 199 people were put to death.

Following the 1930s, the number of executions declined steadily for three decades until they halted for nearly a decade. Between June 3, 1967, and January 17, 1977, no one was executed while the

U.S. Supreme Court evaluated the constitutionality of the death penalty. This *de jure* moratorium was aided by low levels of public support for capital punishment, and there was presumably little political will to carry out executions when the future of capital punishment was in doubt.

In *Furman v. Georgia* (1972), evidence of "arbitrary and discriminatory" sentencing convinced the U.S. Supreme Court that the death penalty, as then administered, violated the Eighth Amendment's prohibition against "cruel and unusual punishment." In *Gregg v. Georgia* (1976) and its companion cases, however, the Court decided that, by restructuring the capital trial and guiding the discretion of jurors, death sentences could be fairly applied. The moratorium on executions ended when convicted murderer Gary Gilmore halted further appeals on his behalf and chose to be executed by a Utah firing squad. Since Gilmore's execution in 1977, more than 200 individuals have been executed—nearly 70% of them in four southern states: Texas, Florida, Louisiana, and Georgia.

Four Trends

The evolution of capital punishment in this country has been marked by at least four discernable trends. The first has been a dramatic reduction in the number and types of crimes punishable by death. Statutory lists of capital crimes have been steadily shortened so that, in most states, they now include only first-degree murder with "special circumstances." Circumstances that define a murder as "death eligible" vary from state to state, but generally include the following: (1) murder committed in the commission of a felony (e.g., robbery, rape, or kidnapping), (2) multiple murder, (3) murder of a police or correctional officer acting in the line of duty, (4) especially cruel or heinous murder, (5) murder for financial gain, (6) murder by an offender having a prior conviction for a violent crime, and (7) causing or directing another to commit murder. Approximately 80% of capital cases involve defendants charged with the first circumstance—murder during the commission of a felony, so-called "felony-murder."

A second trend has been the attempt to reduce the cruelty of executions by replacing one execution technology with another (seemingly more humane) technology. In the 1800s hanging was the most common means of execution. Hanging was eventually replaced by electrocution, then lethal gas, and most recently, lethal injection. As of 1994, 23 states use lethal injection, 12 use electrocution, 7 use lethal gas, 3 use hanging, and 2 use a firing squad. In states that authorize more than one method, the particular method generally is chosen by the condemned prisoner. Although each of these changes in the method of killing was designed to make executions more humane, questions have been raised about the "humaneness" of every method.

A third trend has been the attempt by policymakers to ensure that death sentences are imposed fairly and rationally. To make imposition of the death penalty fairer, courts and legislatures have, at various times, enacted mandatory death sentences for specified crimes, forbidden the practice of mandatory death sentences, broadened the sentencing discretion of jurors, and narrowed the sentencing discretion of jurors. In the opinion of many observers, efforts to increase fairness have failed to produce a fair and rational system of capital punishment. Offenders whose victims are white, for example, and offenders who are sentenced in southern states are still much more likely to be sentenced to death.

A fourth trend involves what might be called the sanitizing of executions. In the 1700s and early 1800s, executions were frequently held as public events witnessed by hundreds of rowdy spectators. A carnival atmosphere prevailed, and the day's festivities often included several hangings. Execution was swift, often occurring only days or weeks after conviction. In contrast, today's executions are conducted late at night, using well-defined and specialized procedures. These modern events are witnessed by only a handful of observers (e.g., journalists, relatives of the condemned prisoner, relatives of the victim) and occur, on average, eight years and five months after conviction. Michael Kroll has argued that this well-intentioned regulation of our system of capital punishment (and even euphemisms such as capital punishment) has had the secondary effect of enabling people to psychologically distance themselves from the act of killing.

The Death Penalty Today

A cursory examination of recent trends—including the number of condemned prisoners, recent Supreme Court decisions, the perception of public support for executions, and the resumption of executions in some states—might lead us to expect a dramatic rise in the rate of executions over the next decade. There has been a steep rise in the number of persons under sentence of death from 1977 through the end of 1993. In 1994, there were more than 2800 convicted prisoners on death row—more than at any time in U.S. history. Roughly 250 people are added to death row each year, and in recent years, the U.S. Supreme Court has consistently rejected legal challenges to the death penalty. At least on the surface, public support for the death penalty remains high—more than 70% of Americans say they favor some form of capital punishment. Finally, although some states have carried out executions without interruption since 1977, the execution chambers of other states are in use again after remaining idle for more than a quarter century. In 1992, Robert Alton Harris became the first person in 25 years to be executed by the state of California and, in 1993, Wesley Alan Dodd became the first person in 29 years to be executed by the state of Washington.

If these trends signal a dramatic rise in the number of executions in the United States, we will see frequent accounts in the media of state-sanctioned hangings, shootings, electrocutions, gassings, and lethal injections. Americans will be forced to confront the death penalty as practice rather than as abstract principle. However, partly owing to a reluctance to face the prospect of frequent executions, some observers have argued that, despite current trends, the often predicted surge in executions will never materialize. S.R. Gross argues that there will probably be no significant increase in the pace of executions:

> Appearances to the contrary notwithstanding, the death penalty we have is pretty much the death penalty we want. The costs of the process are mostly hidden from view. Politicians and judges grumble about delays, but the system does produce what the public demands: a widely available death penalty that is rarely carried out.

Our current system of frequent death sentences but infrequent executions allows us to preserve the symbolism of capital punishment without having to witness a bloodbath.

Even if the rate of executions remains slow and steady, politicians and those seeking political office are likely to keep capital punishment in the forefront of public debate. The issue of capital punishment can be easily and effectively exploited for political gain. Indeed, it has been a key issue in recent presidential elections and state gubernatorial races. Along with other symbolic issues, a candidate's position on the death penalty has been used increasingly to define candidates to voters. Politicians have enthusiastically embraced the death penalty and have frequently proposed that its use be expanded to a host of new crimes. . . .

Too often, declarations of support for capital punishment by politicians are largely symbolic—intended to capitalize on legitimate public outrage over violent crime and to portray the candidate as tough on crime. As Senator Thomas Dasschule of South Dakota has observed, "We debate in codes, like the death penalty as a code for toughness on crime . . . he who gets the code first wins." This cynical manipulation of capital punishment trivializes the public's deep concern over violent crime in America. Unfortunately, the political debate has bypassed a critical discussion of the costs and benefits associated with the death penalty. . . .

The American System of Capital Jurisprudence

When a defendant has been charged with a capital crime, a capital trial ensues. Capital trials are unique in several respects. First, capital jurors must be "death qualified." Death qualification occurs during jury selection. In addition to routine questions about attitudes and personal experiences thought to be pertinent to the case, prospective capital jurors are asked if they will be able to consider a death sentence if the defendant is found guilty of a capital crime. In 1985, the U.S. Supreme Court ruled that potential jurors whose beliefs "substantially impair" their ability to impose a death sentence should be excused from jury service. Judges may also dismiss potential jurors who, in the judgment of the court, exhibit attitudes that substantially interfere with their ability to follow the law. From the pool or death-qualified jurors, prosecuting and defense attorneys challenge and attempt to exclude jurors who they perceive to be unsympathetic to their case.

The structure of the capital trial is also unique. Capital trials are "bifurcated" or split into two phases—a guilt phase and a penalty phase. If a defendant is found guilty of a capital crime in the first phase, then an appropriate sentence is selected in the second "penalty" phase. In the penalty phase, jurors hear testimony pertaining to aggravating and mitigating factors that bear on the circumstances of the offense or the character of the offender. Most states permit the sentencer to render a verdict of death only if aggravating factors outweigh mitigating factors. In all but seven states, the jury makes the final sentencing decision.

Appellate review in capital cases is uniquely complex and elaborate. Capital trials that culminate in a death sentence are automatically appealed to the state supreme court. This direct appeal—circumventing all lower appellate courts—is unique to capital cases. State supreme courts evaluate whether there were legal or constitutional errors at trial, and some states provide for a "proportionality review." In such reviews, the court determines if a particular death sentence is consistent with sentences imposed in similar cases. If the court affirms both the conviction and the sentence, the defendant can file a petition for *certiorari* to the U.S. Supreme Court. This is a request for the case to be heard by the high court based on issues raised in the direct appeal. The Supreme Court rarely grants such requests because an important constitutional issue must be at stake.

If the defendant's direct appeal is unsuccessful, further state and federal appeals are possible. These *habeas corpus* appeals can raise issues that go beyond the trial record including newly discovered evidence, fairness of the capital trial, impartiality of the jury, tainted evidence, incompetence of defense counsel, and prosecutorial misconduct. If these appeals are denied by the trial court, they may be filed with a district court of appeals. State habeas corpus appeals can proceed to the state supreme court and, if denied, a new petition for certiorari can be filed with the U.S. Supreme Court.

After exhausting state appeals, a defendant can file federal habeas corpus petitions. Appeals to federal courts must be confined to alleged violations of constitutional rights. Such rights include the right to due process (Fourteenth Amendment), the prohibition against cruel and unusual punishment (Eighth Amendment), and the right to effective assistance of counsel (Sixth Amendment). Federal appeals begin in a U.S. District Court and then, if denied, are taken to a Circuit Court of Appeals. Finally, appeals may be made to the U.S. Supreme Court on constitutional grounds. Though many forms of appeal are possible after sentencing, only the automatic review by the state supreme court is mandatory.

When a sentence has been upheld by the state supreme court, an execution warrant may be issued. The date of execution is generally set for not less than 30 days after the warrant has been issued. If appeals are pending, the defendant must apply for a stay of execution. Several warrants may be issued and several stays granted before the defendant exhausts all appeals. The power to stay executions and commute death sentences typically rests with a state's governor or a Board of Pardons and Paroles. . . .

The Financial Cost of the Death Penalty

Many Americans support capital punishment because they believe it is cheaper to execute a condemned prisoner than to imprison that person for the remainder of his or her natural life. Indeed, some capital jurors report that one of their reasons for imposing a death sentence is the higher cost of life imprisonment. On its face, this belief seems reasonable—surely by killing condemned prisoners we save years or even decades of costs associated with maintenance. Despite the intuitive appeal of the cheaper-to-execute notion, it is false.

To be sure, the cost of life imprisonment without parole (LWOP)— the alternative to a death sentence in most states—is very high. A full accounting of the cost of LWOP must include construction, financing, and operation costs of a maximum security cell. The annualized costs of building and operating such a cell are approximately $5000, and the cost of maintaining a maximum-security prisoner is approximately $20,000 per year. Taking into account the average age of incarceration for someone convicted of homicide and the average life expectancy for males in the U.S., R. Paternoster has estimated that the total cost of LWOP ranges from $750,000 to $1.1 million. Actual costs, however, may be substantially lower because of the value of prison labor:

> Offenders serving life without parole terms are, and could more extensively be, employed in the institution itself or in prison industries. Inmates working in the prison could perform many of the requisite maintenance and custodial duties, thus reducing employment costs of the prison. Other inmates could be employed in prison industries producing a commodity. These inmates are not paid the full value of their labor so that the institution earns a profit from their work. This directly helps to

reduce the cost of the prison. In addition, inmates serving life terms who work could have a portion of their wages deducted and used to provide restitution for the families of their victims. In many ways, then, murderers sentenced to life terms could help defray the cost of their own imprisonment.

The idea of imprisonment plus restitution appeals strongly to the American public. In a series of recent surveys in several states, respondents were asked to compare the death penalty to alternative sentences. In each case, a majority of respondents preferred sentences of LWOP to the death penalty *if* imprisonment included financial restitution to the families of victims.

Although the cost of LWOP is high, the cost of capital punishment is far higher. It is estimated that California taxpayers could save $90 million annually by abolishing the death penalty. In New York, the Department of Correctional Services has estimated that reinstating the death penalty would cost the state $118 million each year.

Even the cost of trying and executing a single person is enormous. In Florida, the average cost is $3.2 million. In Wisconsin, the Legislative Fiscal Bureau has estimated that reinstating the death penalty would cost the state between $1.6 million and $3.3 million per execution. In California, capital trials are six times more expensive than other murder trials, and in Texas each capital case costs taxpayers an average of $2.3 million—about three times the cost of imprisonment in a maximum security cell for 40 years.

In the most carefully conducted investigation of cost to date, P.J. Cook and D.B. Slawson collected data on cost for each phase of the legal process in North Carolina. They found that, compared to first-degree murder cases in which the death penalty is not sought, the *extra* cost of adjudicating a capital case through to execution is $2.16 million. Of course, we spend time as well as money. Both the California and Florida supreme courts spend nearly half their time reviewing death penalty cases. Clearly, any benefits Americans receive from maintaining a system of capital punishment come at a high price.

Why the Death Penalty Is So Costly

As explained above, capital trials are more complex and time-consuming than other criminal trials at every phase of the legal process—pretrial, jury selection, trial, and appeals. A competently conducted capital trial is preceded by a thorough investigation of both the crime and the offender. Due to the added dimension of the penalty phase, pretrial investigators attempt to locate and interview anyone who may be able to offer testimony that can serve as mitigating evidence (e.g., members of the defendant's family, friends, co-workers, neighbors, and teachers). The personal history of the defendant is often painstakingly reconstructed in order to explain the defendant's crime. M.

Garey has estimated that investigations in capital cases take three to five times longer than noncapital investigations and frequently take as long as two years to complete. The use of various experts—mental health professionals, polygraphers, medical experts, forensic scientists, and jury selection consultants—also add to the costs. Finally, pretrial motions (i.e., requests) are numerous and complex. Capital cases typically involve the filing of two to six times as many motions as noncapital cases.

The process of selecting jurors also takes longer in capital trials. Few prospective jurors are able and willing to commit themselves to participating in a trial that may last for many weeks. The requirement of death qualification lengthens *voir dire* because, even when prospective jurors express distaste for the death penalty, the defense can further question those jurors to demonstrate that their distaste does not prevent them from carrying out their duties. Attorneys in capital cases are usually allotted more peremptory challenges (juror excusals that require no stated reason) and given greater latitude in questioning potential jurors. In many states jurors are questioned individually so their answers will not influence other potential jurors. Finally, it should be remembered that jurors are being selected for both a guilt phase and a penalty phase. As a consequence of these factors, jury selection takes about five times longer in capital trials than in noncapital trials.

Attorneys in capital cases must investigate and prepare for a charge of first-degree murder *and* other charges that qualify the offense as capital (e.g., rape or robbery). Because of the enormous work load, defense and prosecution teams usually include two attorneys and numerous investigators. The efforts of the prosecution and defense teams are further complicated by the necessity of formulating a guilt phase strategy that articulates with a penalty phase strategy. Capital guilt phases consume 10–20 times as many labor hours as noncapital cases, and capital trials as a whole generally last three times longer than comparable noncapital trials. Most important, the extra costs associated with capital trials are incurred not only when a defendant is sentenced to death but *also* when a defendant is acquitted or sentenced to life imprisonment. Not all capital offenders are sentenced to death—estimates range from less than 25% to only 10%. Consequently, many of the dollars spent to maintain a system of capital punishment are spent on the expensive trials of defendants who are never sentenced to death.

The elaborate appeals process for capital cases also is expensive. Cost estimates for appealing a single capital case range from $170,000 to $219,000. Capital appeals generally cost more than noncapital appeals because of the complexity of the legal issues, the number of different issues that can be raised, and the availability of multiple avenues for appeal. Because many appeals are successful and because the defendant's life is at stake, there is ample incentive for pursuing appeals. When an appeal is successful, the state must bear the cost of fighting the death sentence *and* the cost of life imprisonment. Last, the price tag for capital punishment includes the considerable expense of maintaining and operating death rows and execution chambers.

The true cost of the death penalty looms even larger when one considers what economists call "opportunity costs" (i.e., the value of what could have been purchased if X had not been purchased). Put differently, the tremendous sums of money expended each year to maintain a system of capital punishment could be more productively spent elsewhere—for example, on programs designed to prevent or reduce crime. In recent years, many states have been forced to take extraordinary steps to deal with shrinking budgets. Early intervention and education programs have been cut, and violent offenders have been released early from prisons. Yet capital punishment has been spared by budget cutters, perhaps because of its power as a symbol in American society. As in other areas of public policy, by focusing on punishing a few individual offenders, we may be diverting attention and resources away from fundamental structural reforms that address the causes of violent crime.

THE REVIVAL OF THE AMERICAN DEATH PENALTY

Tom Philips

In the following selection, Tom Philips explains that the U.S. Supreme Court ruled in 1972 that the death penalty was unconstitutional. However, he writes, this decision was overturned in 1976, and since that time the number of annual executions performed in the United States has greatly increased. Philips suggests that the effort to "civilize" executions through the use of lethal injections has played a crucial role in maintaining support for capital punishment in America. Additionally, he explores how the death penalty debate has been affected by abolitionist groups such as Amnesty International and the United Nations Human Rights Commission, which advocate a worldwide ban on executions. Philips is a freelance writer who is working on a book about the history and literature of the death penalty.

On 17 January 1977, Gary Gilmore, a convicted double murderer, was strapped into a chair in a warehouse in Utah State Prison and executed by firing squad. Few other executions in the twentieth century have attracted so much attention. Camera crews and reporters swarmed. Every detail of Gilmore's case was scrutinised. Publicists and lawyers fought over the rights to his story. Sacco and Vanzetti in the 1920s and the 'Atom Spies', Julius and Ethel Rosenberg, in the 1950s had made the headlines and inspired poems and plays but only Gary Gilmore got to become the subject of a Pulitzer Prize–winning book by Norman Mailer. In *The Executioner's Song,* Mailer turns Gilmore into the archetypal rootless 'white trash' loser, but the media's interest in Gilmore was more prosaic: his execution brought to an end a four-year hiatus in the use of capital punishment in the United States.

This hiatus began in 1972 when the Supreme Court ruled that, because its use was 'capricious and arbitrary', the death penalty was unconstitutional. Electric chairs, scaffolds and gas chambers started gathering dust. In 1976, however, the decision was overturned. It became a question of waiting to see which capital jurisdiction would become the first to execute a prisoner. Gary Gilmore forced the issue

Excerpted from "Capital Punishment Revival," by Tom Philips, *Contemporary Review,* vol. 272, no. 1587, April 1998. Reprinted with permission from *Contemporary Review.*

to a crisis and, with some reluctance, the state of Utah ushered in a new era in the history of American capital punishment.

As it turned out, no one else was executed after Gilmore for more than two years but a precedent had been set. His execution showed that it was politically safe to go back to using the death penalty. Condemned prisoners could no longer count on receiving an almost indefinite stay of execution. The abolitionist argument appeared to lose credibility. What grounds could there be for protest when a murderer had insisted that the state put him to death? Although Gilmore only cared about what happened to himself, he nevertheless became a *cause célèbre*—the pro–capital punishment lobby's first and only martyr.

By the early 1980s the return to capital punishment was gathering momentum. In 1984, twenty-one people were executed—more than four times as many as in the previous year. Execution technology was changing, too. States began switching to a method which resembled a medical procedure: the lethal injection.

Sanitizing the Death Penalty

For the twenty states which have adopted it, the attractions of this method are obvious. In theory at least, the condemned simply goes to sleep; the executioners simply press a button; and the public simply do not hear so many horror stories from the execution chamber. The prisoner is a patient. Execution becomes euthanasia. What could be more 'civilised' than that?

In the United States, the desire to 'civilise' or, more accurately, sanitize capital punishment dates back to the late nineteenth century. As Jesse James gave way to Henry James, the frontier justice of the lynch-mob and the posse no longer accorded with the nation's image of itself. A new civilisation needed new execution technologies. The sanitization process began.

A similar process had already transformed capital punishment in Europe. France's guillotine offered one solution to the problem of despatching criminals as swiftly as possible while, in Britain, the 'long drop' method of hanging supposedly caused instant painless death. In the United States, neither of these methods won much support. Instead, a number of unlikely mechanisms—including a spring-loaded gallows which broke a prisoner's neck by catapulting him into the air—were tested but abandoned before a commission set up by Governor Hill of New York came up with the idea of electrocution. Shortly afterwards, the first electric chairs were installed and, on 6 August 1890, William Kemmler was electrocuted in front of twenty-five witnesses in Auburn prison. It took two large applications of current to ensure that he was dead but the authorities considered the execution a success. For the first half of the twentieth century, the Chair was widely regarded as a humane and efficient apparatus. Only the gas chamber—first used in 1924 in Nevada—offered any real challenge to its status as the most advanced execution technology.

During the 1970s, however,the Chair's reputation declined. The list of executions which had gone gruesomely wrong was growing. Even when several shocks are not required, the side-effects of electrocution—charred flesh, burnt hair and burst eyeballs—are appalling. Since the gas chamber, too, was tainted by reports of prolonged and painful deaths, the lethal injection seemed a promising alternative. On 7 December 1982, Texas became the first state to use it when Charles Brooks was executed in the 'Death House' at Huntsville Prison.

The Process of Death

At first sight, administering a lethal injection seems a straightforward procedure. Vets do it all the time. In practice, however, it is as elaborate as any other method of execution. Because of this, several states have invested in a computerised machine which releases the three chemicals required—sodium pentothol, pancuronium bromide and potassium chloride—at carefully specified intervals.

The complexity of the appeals system means that a stay is often issued only hours, sometimes minutes, before a prisoner is due to die but once execution looks certain prison officials begin to prepare the prisoner, the chamber and themselves. Every detail is planned and rehearsed. The prisoner is kept under continual surveillance on 'death-watch' in a special holding cell where he—and the vast majority of the three thousand prisoners currently on Death Row are men—has access to his lawyer, his spiritual adviser and, until the last few hours, his family. Before being taken to the chamber, he is given a medical examination—he must be passed fit for execution—a shower and a final meal. In most states, a last cigarette is no longer permitted. Smoking, after all, causes death.

Although the exact protocols governing executions vary, the prisoner generally arrives in the chamber half an hour before receiving the lethal injection. He is strapped onto a specially adapted hospital trolley or gurney. A vein is found and an IV line is attached. Since many condemned prisoners are also intravenous drug users, this is not always an easy task. An official explains each stage of the procedure to the prisoner who, as soon as the line is secure, is covered to the neck with a blanket. The phone-lines are checked to make sure a last minute stay has not been granted. Behind a screen, a doctor monitors the prisoner's heartbeat. A few minutes before the chemicals are released, the blinds on the chamber windows are opened. The state witnesses and the prisoner's 'guests' are allowed to see in. The death warrant is read out. In states with a computerised machine, the executioners prepare the control unit and when the order to proceed is given, two buttons—one active, one dummy—are pressed. The plungers sink in sequence and their contents are released into the IV line. Ideally, the prisoner loses consciousness almost immediately and can be pronounced dead within a matter of minutes. The blinds are drawn. The witnesses are shown out. The corpse is fingerprinted before being handed over to the coroner. The prison governor holds a press conference. Outside the prison, the rival groups of demonstrators begin to go home.

Inevitably, not every execution runs smoothly. In Texas, technicians took forty minutes to insert the IV line in Stephen Morin's vein, had to make running repairs to the equipment while Raymond Landry lay half-dead on the gurney, and administered an incorrect mixture of chemicals to Stephen McCoy. Since a paralysing agent is the first chemical to be injected, the prisoner cannot show any signs of suffering. Who knows if lethal injection is painless or not?

Executions Are Growing More Common

In the United States, the sanitization of capital punishment has played a crucial role in maintaining public support. Certainly, there is no evidence to suggest that the capital jurisdictions are becoming reluctant to execute offenders. Texas broke its own record when Michael Lockhart became the thirty-seventh person to be executed there in 1997. No other American state in the twentieth century has put to death so many people in any one year. In February 1998, Karla Tucker became the first woman to be executed in Texas for more than a century.

Not that the United States is the only country to practise capital punishment, of course. Despite the growing strength of the abolitionist movement at every level, just over half the world's nations retain it and, although it is sometimes difficult to get accurate figures, reports suggest that many of these are now carrying out executions more frequently than they were a decade ago.

In several Islamic countries, for example, executions—many of which are carried out in public—have become increasingly common. Saudi Arabia executed an average of about ten people a month in 1997 while in Iran the number of executions doubled between 1995 and 1996. In Afghanistan, shortly before its defeat by Taliban forces in 1996, the government began a series of public hangings to demonstrate its commitment to Koranic law. The new regime has continued and extended this practice. An Afghan woman accused of talking in public with a man from outside her family can expect to receive the death penalty—as can anyone caught watching television.

In China, criminals are regularly executed for offences which, in many other countries, would warrant little more than a short prison term and any government initiative to launch a 'clamp-down on crime' is generally accompanied by news of a spectacular mass execution such as the one carried out in the early 1990s when hundreds of petty offenders were shot. The enthusiastic use of capital punishment by the Taiwanese government is also causing concern.

Even in countries where the death penalty fell out of favour for several years, the authorities have returned to capital punishment. Until six people were hanged there in 1997, there had not been an execution in Burundi since 1982. Now more than two hundred people are awaiting execution. The number of governments which have even bothered to discuss the possibility of abolition in recent years has been tiny.

The reasons behind this resurgence in capital punishment vary from society to society. The hangings in Burundi were essentially acts of revenge for the massacres of 1993. In the Middle East, fundamentalism has inspired a move towards penal codes based on strict religious law. In the United States, a widespread fear of crime, coupled with the belief that only traditional disciplinary solutions—such as the death penalty—can cure society's ills, has forced liberal abolitionism onto the defensive. President Bill Clinton himself openly endorses the use of the death penalty and in 1992 he interrupted his presidential campaign so that he could return to Arkansas and, as State Governor, refuse to grant a last minute reprieve to a lobotomised man who did not even understand the meaning of the word 'execution'. The possibility of televising executions has been seriously discussed on several occasions.

A Question of Human Rights

Somewhat paradoxically, however, this resurgence has been accompanied by an equally obvious upsurge in abolitionism. Opposition to the death penalty has not been silenced and organisations such as Amnesty International and the United Nations Human Rights Commission are calling for a total, world-wide ban.

Fifty years ago, the Universal Declaration of Human Rights, issued by the United Nations on 10 December 1948, left the question open to interpretation. Article 5 states that 'No one shall be subjected to torture or to cruel, inhuman or degrading punishment' but whether or not capital punishment falls into this category depends entirely on what is meant by cruel, inhuman or degrading. The idealistic spirit of the Declaration as a whole suggests that it does but, as subsequent debate has shown, there are plenty of people willing to argue that it does not. Such ambiguity was, at the time, inevitable. In 1948, most of the major powers—including Britain—retained the death penalty and none of them were likely to condemn their own penal practises as violations of human rights.

Since then, however, other international initiatives—the International Covenant of Civil and Political Rights, the European Convention on Human Rights—have taken a stronger line and the recognition that capital punishment constitutes a violation appears to be accepted more widely than at any other time. Whilst voluntary protocols and treaties do not carry much weight with governments intent on retaining the death penalty, they do at least mean that abolitionists can supplement the language of compassion with the terminology of human rights.

The British government, too, appears to be taking the issue more seriously. Shortly after it was elected, the new Labour administration announced that it would be pursuing an 'ethical' foreign policy and would not do business with regimes which abused the rights of their citizens. Likewise, the British media—which usually only deals with the subject when a high profile public figure such as the Nigerian writer Ken Saro-Wiwa is executed—has given unprecedented coverage to capital punishment. In the summer of 1997, in particular, the plight of the two British nurses accused of murder in Saudi Arabia provoked a sustained and understandable outcry. Under *Sharia* law, unless a victim's family accepts a 'blood money' payment, the punishment for murder is death. For several months, it seemed possible that both Deborah Parry and Lucille McLauchlan would suffer a bloody public decapitation outside Damman Prison in a place known locally as 'Chop Square'. Articles denouncing *Sharia* law regularly appeared in the press and the government was urged to exert diplomatic pressure on the Saudi authorities.

What rapidly emerged from this coverage, however, was that it wasn't the idea of capital punishment *per se* which most commentators found distressing but the specific practises sanctioned by *Sharia* law. The death penalty wasn't a problem: execution by sword in a public square was. If Deborah Parry and Lucille McLauchlan had faced the possibility of being injected with lethal chemicals in Texas or Missouri, the response of the government and the public would have undoubtedly been more restrained.

This, I suppose, should come as no surprise. For most of the twentieth century, attitudes towards capital punishment have been distorted by the myth that there are two distinct categories of execution—the barbaric and the civilised—and that there are qualitative differences between them. Just as, in certain circumstances a 'terrorist' can become a 'freedom fighter', an act which would otherwise be an atrocity can be disguised as judicial execution. Yet the refinements which allegedly differentiate public decapitation from lethal injection are merely procedural details. The end is the same even if the means have been sanitized. The difference between the two categories is merely aesthetic.

A Powerful Revenge

Perhaps the most significant development in the recent history of capital punishment, however, has been the collapse of the rationalist defence that the death penalty is the ultimate deterrent. In the face of overwhelming evidence that it has no impact whatsoever on the crime rate, its supporters have had to resort to the more primitive argument of revenge. At the same time, the arguments for abolitionism—which, in the eighteenth and nineteenth centuries, originally grew out of an emotional, almost sentimental reaction to the brutalities of the scaffold—have become increasingly rational: the death penalty is ineffective, arbitrary and, in the case of a 'mistake', irreversible. It is not an act of justice. It is a political act by which regimes seek to demonstrate power. Moreover, it is not even cost-effective. In the United States it costs twice as much to execute someone as it does to imprison them for life.

Nevertheless, progress towards global abolition has been slow. Until the world's most powerful nation, the United States, and the most populous, China, renounce the death penalty, international initiatives to abolish it will continue to pass by unnoticed. Even with its 'ethical' foreign policy, the British government is unlikely to jeopardise the 'special relationship' by ending its silence on American executions.

THE UNDYING PROBLEM OF THE DEATH PENALTY

Hiller B. Zobel

Hiller B. Zobel is a Fellow of the Society of American Historians and a judge on the Massachusetts Superior Court. In the following article, Zobel discusses some of the controversies that have surrounded the death penalty in America since its inception. Historically, he writes, the courts have viewed the death penalty with some misgivings, debating whether it is fair, humane, and effective in deterring crime. Zobel concludes that the death penalty is inseparably linked with revenge and therefore must be carefully regulated by the legal system.

Chief Justice Oliver Wendell Holmes of the Massachusetts Supreme Judicial Court spent part of May 6, 1901, writing about the death penalty, and specifically about electrocution. Earlier that day lawyers for Luigi Storti, a twenty-seven-year-old Italian laborer without a family in America, convicted for the murder of a fellow immigrant in Boston's North End, had argued that electrocution was punishment "cruel or unusual," proscribed by the Massachusetts Declaration of Rights, a charter nine years older than the federal Bill of Rights.

Until 1898 the mode of capital punishment in Massachusetts, as in almost every other state that inflicted death, had been the gallows. The electric chair was supposed to eliminate the uncertainty and pain of hanging (where miscalculation of the "drop" distance might result in slow strangulation or ripping the head from the body), with the aid of the nineteenth century's secular deity, science, and that newly harnessed miracle, electricity.

Although Storti was to be the first person ever to die in Massachusetts's electric chair, he naturally cared less about the method of execution than about mere survival. His lawyers' first move after the guilty verdict had been a straightforward review by the Massachusetts high court focusing on claims of legal error, such as that the statements he had made to the police were not voluntary. That appeal had failed, and so had an effort to obtain an executive commutation and a legislative attempt to abolish the death penalty completely. Then,

Reprinted from "The Undying Problem of the Death Penalty," by Hiller B. Zobel, *American Heritage*, vol. 48, no. 8, December 1997. Reprinted by permission of *American Heritage* magazine, a division of Forbes, Inc. Copyright © by Forbes, Inc., December 1997.

days before his execution, Storti developed pulmonary hemorrhages, probably from tuberculosis, that left him so weak he would have to be carried to the electric chair. Unwilling to execute a dying man—and hoping for a natural death that would solve everyone's problems—Gov. Murray Crane stayed the execution until May 11.

Then Storti's health began to improve, and his lawyers presented the petition that Holmes and his colleagues had just considered. With less than a week remaining before execution, Holmes—a fast worker under any circumstances—set out the Court's views promptly so that, as he put it, "we may avoid delaying the course of the law and raising false hopes in [Storti's] mind."

The planned execution, Storti's lawyers had argued, was cruel or unusual punishment because the procedure involved not only pain and death but also psychological anguish. No, replied Holmes, electrocution was "devised for the purpose of reaching the end proposed as swiftly and painlessly as possible." Any mental suffering, he added, "is due not to its being more horrible to be struck by lightning than to be hanged with the chance of slowly strangling, but to the general fear of death. The suffering due to that fear the law does not seek to spare. It means that it shall be felt." Holmes was merely saying in his elegant, direct way that the death penalty sought as much to deter future criminals as to punish current ones.

Storti's lawyers immediately petitioned for a federal writ of habeas corpus, this time arguing that Storti's detention somehow violated a treaty between Italy and the United States. Impatiently the federal circuit court in Boston denied the petition and even (as lower federal judges were permitted to do) prohibited the right to appeal to the United States Supreme Court.

Undaunted, counsel for Storti persuaded United States Supreme Court Justice Horace Gray to allow the appeal to proceed, meanwhile lodging another appeal, which Holmes quickly rejected, arguing that irreconcilable laws were requiring both "special" and "solitary" confinement before execution. On December 2, 1901, the Supreme Court permanently ended Storti's procedural odyssey. The grounds purporting to justify Storti's release, said Justice David Brewer for a unanimous Court, were "wholly without foundation." He called the case "another of the numerous instances" in which applications and appeals were taken "quite destitute of meritorious grounds, and operating only to delay the administration of justice."

It is difficult to tell whether the exertions on Storti's behalf drew their inspiration from the death penalty itself or from the fearsome new technology. New York had enacted the first electrocution statute in 1888, responding to the report of a special commission that it represented "the most humane and practical method known to modern science of carrying into effect the sentence of death."

We tend to consider misgivings about the death penalty a late-twentieth-century concern. In fact, in 1794 Pennsylvania abolished death as a punishment for all crimes except "willful, deliberate, and premeditated" killing. Even earlier, in the colonies as in Britain, the courts had applied a concept called "benefit of clergy" to decapitalize manslaughter—that is, killing without malice. In medieval England clerics could insist on being tried in ecclesiastical courts; they proved their status by demonstrating literacy (because, generally, only they knew how to read). Later the "benefit" became available to any demonstrated reader. By 1707 even an illiterate first offender could escape the noose, after being branded on the thumb to preclude any subsequent application. Louisiana passed an abolitional legislative resolution in 1830 and revoked it in 1846. Also in 1846 Michigan abolished capital punishment for all crimes but treason; in 1853 Wisconsin abolished it absolutely.

Other states tried to deal with the problem by giving the jury power to recommend against death. It became common also to classify murder by degrees. Typically, first-degree murder entailed not only malice—unjustified killing—but also premeditation, defined, not very helpfully, as reflection, even if for only a few seconds, followed by the decision to kill and then by the killing. In essence, the jury could decide life or death according to its own view of the facts, and in all cases, of course, the jurors retained the unsanctioned but uncontrollable right to disregard even compelling evidence and acquit: jury nullification. As Holmes said in another context, jurors can "let a little popular prejudice into the administration of law (in violation of their oath)." Indeed, repeated demonstrations of jurors' reluctance to render a verdict that would mandate the death sentence led, as early as the 1830s, to an editorial lament in a Rhode Island newspaper with an unintended irony: "Unless the prisoner, from his color or extraction, is cut off from ordinary sympathy, he is almost sure of an acquittal."

The fact is that, historically, we have never regarded the death penalty placidly. Curtis Bok, a judge in Pennsylvania on both the trial and the appellate benches, once asked, "Why is the State so ashamed of its process that it must kill at dead of night in an isolated place and on an unnamed day?" The man who pulls the switch generally stands hidden from everyone's view. When Storti died, the press account pointedly noted the anonymity of the executioner. Even when death comes by a firing squad, the round in one of the rifles is blank, presumably so that no one will know for certain that his was a fatal shot.

The death penalty provokes in us dreadfully conflicted feelings, beginning with recognition of the need for a fair procedure in determining guilt and imposing punishment. Like Francis Bacon four centuries ago, we know that "revenge is a kind of wild justice, which the more man's nature runs to, the more ought law to weed it out." Thus we recoil from lynch law, either in fact (Leo Frank and Emmett Till) or in fiction (*The Ox-Bow Incident*).

Yet even as we insist on due process, we express impatience with the inhibitions that fair procedure imposes. In part an appellate court's role is to restrain the mob spirit; still, what judges see as ensuring constitutional and legal rights, the public and the victim's family often denounce as legal technicalities. Certainly, when a client's life is at stake, a good, honest lawyer will try every available argument, just as Storti's did. Hope does ever bloom; remember, too, what Samuel Johnson once advised Boswell: "An argument which does not convince yourself, may convince the judge to whom you urge it." It was also Johnson who said, "When a man knows he is to be hanged in a fortnight, it concentrates his mind [and, one might add, his lawyer's mind] wonderfully."

Counsel's ingenuity and desperate effort do not always sit well with the appellate courts. Justice Brewer's impatience with Storti has found echoes in our own time, when Supreme Court justices have expressed similar unhappiness with not only defendants and lawyers but also some lower court judges. Nonetheless the Court as an institution and the justices themselves have found the implications of the death penalty not so easy to fathom. *Furman v. Georgia*, the 1972 decision that for a time eliminated executions in this country, produced no fewer than nine separate opinions, one per justice: five concurring with the one-page anonymous per curiam order, four dissenting. Two of the "majority" justices thought the death penalty cruel and unusual punishment per se; the others thought it unconstitutionally disparate in its effects: Most of those executed were poor, young, ignorant, and perhaps the victims of racial discrimination.

Eight years later, when the Massachusetts Supreme Judicial Court struck down the commonwealth's new *Furman*-shaped death penalty statute, it condemned the psychological agony inherent in the punishment, directly refuting Holmes's tough words to Storti. "Mental pain," Chief Justice Edward Hennessey wrote, quoting Justice Brennan in *Furman*, "is an inseparable part of our practice of punishing criminals by death, for the prospect of pending execution exacts a frightful toll during the inevitable long wait between the imposition of sentence and the actual infliction of death." Of course, part of the waiting period results from the drawnout appellate process.

If the mental-pain view prevails, no form of execution can ever pass constitutional muster. After all, even lethal injection, supposedly the most painless method, still involves the "long wait" following conviction while the legal process tries to ensure that death, the one punishment not subject to revision, comes only to the truly guilty. And electrocution, whose supposed absence of pain so attracted the Victorians, has turned out to hold its own horrors. Lewis E. Lawes, for many years the warden at Sing Sing Prison, had this to say about what happens in the electric chair: "The [prisoner] leaps as if to break the strong leather straps that hold [him]. Sometimes a thin wisp of smoke pushes itself out from under the helmet that holds the head electrode, followed by a faint odor of burning flesh. [The body heats to 130 degrees—a little less than rare roast beef.] The hands turn red, then white, and the cords of the neck stand out like steel bands."

The newspaper account of Storti's death omitted some of the details, but the reporter had certainly seen the same sights that Warden Lawes had: "The body of Storti surged up against the tightly buckled straps, which creaked and strained under the pressure, the veins in his neck and wrists and face swelled." Afterward, the reporter wrote, "none of the other witnesses would say anything of particular interest about the execution, except that nothing could be more sudden or certain in producing death than electricity as it is applied in the prison."

Deliberately using the power of the state to take a human life continues to raise moral and political issues that legislators find uncomfortable to face and judges find impossible to solve. Whether today's out-of-sight executions more effectively deter crime than did the public spectacles of hangings in earlier times is not the only question. Over the last twenty years society has become more willing to recognize the interests of victims or (in cases of murder) their families in the punishment process. Elected local prosecutors, when deciding, for example, to explore the possibility of a plea to second-degree murder or manslaughter, pay careful attention to the survivors' desires. Beyond that, at sentencing time, even when the judge has no discretion, many states give family representatives the right to vent their feelings in open court.

In short, although revenge may indeed be a kind of wild justice, we are now coming to think that perhaps the law needs not to root it out but to regulate it. Whether that regulation should involve the latter-day gallows tree is a question that is anything but new, yet that remains and will remain for all of us to ponder and—however we can—answer.

THE SUPREME COURT AND THE DEATH PENALTY

David O. Stewart

In the following selection, David O. Stewart takes a look at the U.S. Supreme Court, which deals with many capital punishment cases that are in appeals and also bears the burden of determining the constitutionality of the death penalty. The court declared the death penalty unconstitutional in 1972 but reversed its decision four years later, he writes. Ironically, Stewart notes, two justices who supported the death penalty in the 1970s later became outspoken critics of capital punishment. He concludes that the controversy surrounding the death penalty will continue to be a serious issue for the Supreme Court. Stewart is a partner in the law firm Ropes and Gray in Washington, D.C.

Term after term, the issue of capital punishment persists on the U.S. Supreme Court's docket, like an unwanted guest who refuses to leave.

Even though its overall caseload has dropped significantly in recent years, death penalty cases remain one of the Court's docket staples.

A Change of Heart

But the real fireworks on capital punishment recently have come from Justice Harry A. Blackmun, who stepped down in 1994, and retired Justice Lewis F. Powell Jr. Both stated publicly that, after many years of voting to sustain capital sentences, they had concluded that the death penalty is unconstitutional.

That position was held for years by their colleagues William J. Brennan Jr., now retired, and the late Thurgood Marshall. But Brennan and Marshall were unabashed liberals whose views on capital punishment often were dismissed as extreme.

Blackmun and Powell were appointed to the Court by President Richard M. Nixon, and could not be mistaken for liberals in criminal cases.

Their change of heart reflects the contradictions and tensions that swirl around capital punishment and the Supreme Court's central role in determining its course in this country.

Reprinted from "Dealing with Death: The Court Cannot Escape the Issue of Capital Punishment," by David O. Stewart, *ABA Journal*, vol. 80, November 1994. Reprinted by permission of *ABA Journal*.

Uncomfortable with Death

The views of Powell and Blackmun contrast starkly with the current popular enthusiasm for the death penalty, which is in effect in 37 states and which Congress approved for a variety of federal offenses listed in the crime bill that President Bill Clinton signed in September 1994.

But the reality is that the death penalty does not often result in actual executions.

Between 1973 and 1992, a total of 4,704 convicted murderers were sentenced to death, but only 188 of them, or 4 percent, were executed. Moreover, 1,815 of those death row prisoners, or 39 percent, succeeded in having their death sentences lifted by various means of judicial review or executive clemency.

Perhaps the most striking statistic is that 451 of those sentenced to die—nearly 10 percent—had their underlying convictions overturned on appeal.

As of the summer of 1994, 2,575 prison inmates languished on death row. The average time between sentencing and execution for the 31 prisoners put to death in 1992 was 114 months, or nine and a half years.

For a nation so evidently smitten with the idea of the death penalty, we seem to be hesitant to carry it out. That discomfort is evident at the Supreme Court.

A Challenge to the Court

The Court's current entanglement with capital punishment began in 1972 with *Furman v. Georgia*, 408 U.S. 238, a challenge to the Georgia death penalty.

Capital punishment was not very popular then. In the five years before that decision, no execution had been carried out on an American prisoner.

The Court voted 5–4 in *Furman* that death penalties were cruel and unusual punishment, which is barred by the Eighth Amendment to the Constitution.

In five separate opinions, the *Furman* majority criticized the complete absence of standards for controlling the imposition of death sentences, making executions random events.

Ironically, both Blackmun and Powell dissented in *Furman*, voting to uphold the death penalty statutes then in force.

But a consensus never developed on the Court that the death penalty itself was unconstitutional, and, in 1976, in seven consolidated cases led by *Gregg v. Georgia*, 428 U.S. 153, the justices approved a number of capital punishment statutes that had been drafted to meet the *Furman* objections.

Since *Gregg*, the Court has struggled to reconcile two conflicting values in its jurisprudence of the death penalty.

On one hand, the justices have sought to assure consistent imposition of capital punishment to prevent unfair discrimination among defendants, which is the teaching of *Furman*.

To achieve the goal, the Court has insisted that capital punishment statutes prescribe careful sentencing procedures and provide guidance for the jury's deliberations.

But the justices also have insisted, as in *Lockett v. Ohio*, 455 U.S. 104 (1982), that defendants cannot be restricted in pleading that their unique circumstances do not justify receiving death sentences.

Both values are grounded in the simple fact that a death sentence is irreversible.

The Finality of Death

As expressed in the joint opinion of Justices Powell, Potter Stewart and John Paul Stevens in *Woodson v. North Carolina*, 428 U.S. 280 (1976), "Death, in its finality, differs more from life imprisonment than a 100-year prison term differs from one of only a year or two."

The finality of a death sentence is particularly unsettling because of other simple facts.

Defendants in capital cases are, for instance, ordinarily poor persons living on the margins of society, and they often receive poor legal representation. In many states, a capital defendant will be represented by a court-appointed lawyer who receives only a few hundred or a few thousand dollars from the state—this to fight the ultimate penalty.

Equally troubling, the prosecutors who decide whether to ask for death, as well as the people on the bench and in the jury box who decide on life or death, are subject to human prejudices and biases.

A physically attractive defendant whose loyal family comes to court every day will be more appealing than an unkempt, unattractive defendant who appears to have no connection to the community.

Is the decision that they live or die based on what they did, or on who they are or how they look?

Race also appears to play a role. In *McClesky v. Kemp*, 481 U.S. 279 (1987), the defendant presented the Baldus Study, which examined 2,000 murder cases in Georgia in the 1970s.

The study concluded that, although the race of the defendant had little apparent impact on whether a death sentence was imposed, defendants who killed white persons were significantly more likely to be sentenced to death than those who killed blacks.

By a 5–4 margin, the Court—in an opinion written by Justice Powell—rejected the Baldus Study as a basis for vacating the death sentence of McClesky, who has since been executed. If the case had gone the other way, capital punishment might have become virtually impossible to implement in this country.

At a practical level, death suffuses the professional life of a modern Supreme Court justice.

During the 1993 term the Court decided four capital cases, and during the first two sittings of the 1994 term, two more were scheduled for argument: *Harris v. Alabama,* No. 93-7659; and *Kyles v. Whitley,* No. 93-7927.

But the decided cases are only the tip of the capital punishment iceberg at the Supreme Court. The justices develop a peculiar intimacy with capital cases.

When a prisoner receives an execution date, the first priority ordinarily is gaining a stay. If the lower courts deny the stay, the prisoner's request often lands at the Supreme Court, often under the intense time pressure of an approaching execution.

Each application is directed to the particular justice responsible for the sentencing jurisdiction. (Those responsibilities are divided among the justices according to the boundaries of the federal circuits.)

The Supreme Court clerk's office distributes a weekly list of scheduled executions to all the justices, and copies of case filings by inmates who have been before the Court previously are made available to them.

Individual justices granted 16 stays out of 70 applications during the 1993 term; the rest were denied. Each justice also may refer a stay request to the entire Court for its review, which occurred 50 times during the 1993 term. Only two of those stays were granted, however.

Through this process, each justice is acutely aware of, and becomes a sort of participant in, most executions.

The long-term effect of this involvement has been described as "the bitter education of the cases" by Powell's biographer, Professor John C. Jeffries Jr. of the University of Virginia School of Law in Charlottesville.

A System Plagued by Doubt

In *Justice Lewis F. Powell, Jr.: A Biography* (New York City: Charles Scribner's Sons, 1994), Jeffries offers this insight into the impact of that education: "After fifteen years of capital cases, Powell knew firsthand their deadly hold on the judge's peace of mind. He knew how hard it was not to take a second, third, or fourth look at rejected claims, how easy it seemed to put the whole thing off for one more hearing, how much courage—or callousness—it took to treat death like any other penalty.

"Some judges could achieve that emotional distance, but Powell came to believe that the system as a whole would always be plagued by doubt and that doubting itself it would inspire resentment and contempt."

Justice Blackmun offered a more passionate explanation of his decision to oppose capital punishment when he dissented in February to the denial of certiorari in *Callins v. Collins,* No. 93-7054.

Explaining that the twin goals of "fairness and rationality" in capital sentencing cannot be achieved, Blackmun wrote:

"From this day forward, I no longer shall tinker with the machinery of death. For more than 20 years I have endeavored—indeed I have struggled—along with a majority of the Court, to develop procedural and substantive rules that would lend more than the mere appearance of fairness to the death penalty endeavor.

"The problem is that the inevitability of factual, legal, and moral error gives us a system that we know must wrongly kill some defendants."

CHAPTER 2

PERSPECTIVES ON THE DEATH PENALTY

ANGER AND AMBIVALENCE

David A. Kaplan

In the following article, David A. Kaplan explores American attitudes about the death penalty. He reports that while most Americans claim to favor the death penalty, overall the country's population has mixed feelings about actually executing people. Although many politicians have vowed to speed up the process of executing death row prisoners, Kaplan writes, the system has remained overwhelmingly backlogged. The long paper trail created by capital trials, the slow appeals process, and arguments between Supreme Court justices over capital punishment have all contributed to the problem, he states. Kaplan is a senior writer for *Newsweek* magazine.

If it's swift punishment you want, you'll love the case of Giuseppe Zangara. Back on Feb. 15, 1933, in the middle of Miami, this slightly deranged malcontent pulled a gun on President-elect Franklin Roosevelt and fired repeatedly. He missed, but mortally wounded the mayor of Chicago. Thirty-three days later—after arrest, guilty plea and sentence—Zangara was electrocuted in Florida's "Old Sparky." In the good old days of capital punishment, there wasn't even enough time to sign a book deal.

The machinery of capital justice cranks a lot more slowly now. Death row is a growth industry. The rare inmate to die hangs on close to 10 years before meeting the executioner. In Florida, triple-killer Gary Alvord is celebrating his 22d year, still hoping, still appealing. Up the interstate, one quarter of Georgia's 109 death-row prisoners have been there since at least 1980. And in Montana, until May 10, Duncan McKenzie had avoided the lethal needle for 20 years. In fact, he fell just one vote short of gaining his eighth stay of execution. He may have been the coldblooded murderer of a schoolteacher, but he had chutzpah. His last argument in court: two decades on death row was itself "cruel and unusual" punishment, and therefore a violation of his constitutional rights. Never mind that McKenzie's lawyers had asked for the prior stays and had helped to create the judicial black hole he found himself in. A federal court didn't buy the claim and within days McKenzie became the first inmate executed in Montana since FDR's third term.

Give or take a few miscreants, there are currently 3,000 inmates on American death rows. That's more by far than at any time in world history. California alone has 407, followed by Texas with 398 and Florida with 342. Yet for each of the last 19 years—ever since the U.S. Supreme Court allowed states to resume capital punishment—no more than about 2 percent of the death-row total has ever been executed. In 1994, the number was 31; this year, the figure might reach 50. Spending a reported annual $90 million on capital cases, California has managed to gas just two inmates—and one of them waived all his appeals.

Capital punishment in America is a paper tiger. Despite tough political bluster and overwhelming poll numbers, the nation is ambivalent about the ultimate penalty. For many years, legislators, governors, judges and victims'-rights activists have vowed to finally get on with it—to bar endless appeals, sanction mollycoddling defense lawyers, root out of office bleeding-heart governors. Congress passed reforms and cut funding for defense lawyers, the U.S. Supreme Court cracked down, and leaders like New York Gov. Mario Cuomo were voted out. The press, *Newsweek* included, proclaimed in various aqueous illusions that the floodgates would soon open or that the logjam was about to be broken.

It's never happened. State prosecutors' offices remain understaffed and overwhelmed, courts have hopelessly long backlogs (assuming they can find lawyers for the defendants in the first place) and juries in most states enthusiastically continue to send killers to death row. For every inmate to die, though, there are five new ones to take his (or, in the rare case, her) cell. To clean up the backlog, states would have to execute a killer a day (Christmas and Easter included) through 2021. Even Texas—far and away the nation's death-penalty capital, with a third of all executions since 1976—manages to dispatch only about one in eight condemned inmates.

At the water cooler and in the streets of Union, S.C., people argue about what fate the Susan Smiths of the world deserve. And race and poverty have never gone away in the vexing national debate over the death penalty. But those moral and ideological questions have now been overshadowed by a simpler fact: people sentenced to death nonetheless live on in prison. What's the most frequent cause of death for death-row inmates? As of 1992, according to the U.S. Bureau of Justice Statistics, electrocution and lethal injection were mere runnerups. The No. 1 killer: "Natural Causes." What becomes of a penal policy that on its face is a sham?

Ask Alex Kozinski, one of the country's most outspoken and conservative federal judges who almost always upholds death sentences. "We have constructed a machine that is extremely expensive, chokes our legal institutions, visits repeated trauma on victims' families and ultimately produces nothing like the benefits we would expect from an effective system of capital punishment," he wrote in a recent, controversial op-ed article in *The New York Times*. "This is surely the worst of all worlds."

The systemic ambivalence about the death penalty is reflected in virtually all the 38 states that have death chambers open for business. During his election campaign last year, South Carolina's new attorney general, Charlie Condon, was so taken with a triple execution in Arkansas that he proposed doing away with his state's electric chair. His reform? An "electric sofa," to juice several inmates at a time. South Carolina's death-row population is 59; its last execution was in 1991. Ambivalence there may best be demonstrated by the Smith verdict itself last week. While polls showed wide support for her execution, it took jurors less than three hours to reach a unanimous verdict to spare her.

New York, after 20 years of abolitionist administrations in Albany, this spring became the newest state with capital punishment on the books. When it will post a job listing for executioners is another matter. It typically takes a decade before all courts sign off on a death statute. New York's is so full of procedural safeguards that some wonder if executions will ever resume. "That new law essentially says, 'KICK ME'," observes law professor Franklin Zimring, of the University of California, Berkeley. "They'll be lucky to have an execution in the *21st* century." In a liberal state like New York, that may be the perfect political outcome for Republican Gov. George Pataki. He got the death penalty out of legislative purgatory, but he'll never actually have to deal with administering it.

That may also be the strategy of Bill Clinton. Already his re-election-campaign spots disingenuously boast of adding dozens of new crimes to the federal death statute. And the U.S. government is busily building its own death row in the Midwest, complete with a $800,000 death chamber, even though currently there are only six federal inmates convicted of capital crimes. Trouble is, federal executions, assuming they even get underway this decade, are unlikely to be more than a criminal-justice blip. The new laws contain such everyday offenses as killing a chicken inspector of the Agriculture Department.

Nobody in the capital-punishment system wants to accept blame for the current stalemate. Prosecutors blame judges, who blame courts, who blame the law, which gets passed down by Supreme Court justices, who don't speak, except to Nina Totenberg on occasion. But the primary whipping boys for execution gridlock have long been defense lawyers. It's true that a ferociously dedicated group of abolitionists, among them David Bruck, Smith's counsel, have fought the death penalty in every venue across the land. The fact is, judges are the ones who grant stays of execution, courts come up with incredibly complex rules and prosecutors don't push cases along. In one Indiana case, the state took two years to transcribe the trial record of a case. In most state A.G.s' offices in the death-belt states, appeals sit around because there aren't enough government lawyers to handle the load.

At the top of the system, the U.S. Supreme Court has labored hard to get out of the death-penalty business. But the justices every year get drawn into a few major cases and wind up having to revise doctrine. Worse, while there are no justices anymore like William Brennan or Thurgood Marshall—who voted against all death sentences all the time—the high court often still splits 5-4 on capital cases, indicating that even the Supremes can't figure things out. That leads to further confusion for lower-court judges, who have enough trouble keeping up with legal changes from two years prior. Chief Judge Gerald Tjoflat of the 11th U.S. Circuit Court of Appeals in Atlanta says that some of his colleagues spend half their time wading through capital cases. "I've been in the judging business for 28 years," Tjoflat says, "and there's nothing harder."

Some judges take an especially long time to make up their minds. In 1986, an Arizona killer named Ruben Zaragoza exhausted his state remedies and appealed to the federal district court in Phoenix. Zaragoza's case hasn't been heard from since. Judge Earl H. Carroll, who has had the case for the last nine years, declined to comment. Two years ago, Arizona Attorney General Grant Woods got so annoyed with slow federal judges in his state that he took an extraordinary step. Woods asked the Ninth U.S. Circuit Court of Appeals, based in San Francisco, to order the judges to rule on 30 cases that had languished for a decade. The appeals court refused. "That was real smart of Arizona," says a deputy attorney general of one Southern state. "Trying to move a federal judge is like trying to make a pig dance. It doesn't work and it annoys the pig."

The Ninth Circuit itself has come under frequent attack from politicians. That court "is the most liberal of the circuits in the United States," complains California Attorney General Dan Lungren. "Some members appear to have a strong bias against the death penalty." Lungren has in mind the notorious case of Robert Alton Harris in 1992 that embarrassed the entire federal judicial system. Harris had been before both the California and the U.S. Supreme Courts six times in his 13 years on San Quentin's death row. On the eve of his scheduled April 21 appointment with the executioner, the Ninth Circuit kept issuing stays and the justices in Washington kept lifting them—into the predawn hours. Finally, an enraged Supreme Court—citing the Ninth Circuit's "civil disobedience"—ordered the circuit judges to abstain from any further interference. Harris was executed in the gas chamber forthwith. The case continues to haunt all participants in the California system.

Lungren correctly notes that the 24-member Ninth Circuit appeals court does in fact have several judges—from both ends of the political spectrum—who consistently vote against death sentences and thereby slow down the tumbrels. But so what? Of California's 407 death-row inmates, only eight have cases pending before the Ninth Circuit. And what of Lungren's own office? Of the state's 407 condemned prisoners, 120 are totally stalled before the state supreme court because there are no defense lawyers for them. (Constitutional law entitles them to representation.) "We haven't appointed counsel for anyone in 1993, 1994 and 1995," says Robert Reichman, a court administrator. "We're on 1992's cases." In short, that means at least three extra years of life and free meals for California's condemned. Capital punishment is about the only area of litigation where there aren't lawyers climbing over each other to earn a fee.

With his considerable political skills, why doesn't Lungren press the state supreme court to find lawyers, or urge the state bar to get members to take their ethics obligations seriously? Or, as one Ninth Circuit judge asked, why doesn't he simply call a press conference to explain why more than one quarter of California's condemned population is no closer to execution now than three years ago when the Ninth Circuit was being pummeled for its handling of the Harris case? "While this may be an area of legitimate concern," Lungren answered in a prepared statement, "we do not have any direct jurisidiction over it and, at a time when my own department is facing cuts of $10 million, it is questionable how much leverage we would have in achieving funding for court-appointed defense lawyers."

Ambivalence is not limited to judges and prosecutors. Earlier this year, the Florida clemency board voted to defer a decision on Danny Doyle—a mentally impaired murderer who was sentenced 13 years earlier—until the year 2020. He'll remain in death-row lockup, says Joe Bizarro, spokesman for the Florida attorney general. Jurors, too, seem to have mixed feelings. In 1987, Louisiana's electric chair got humming. It claimed four lives in one nine-day period and four more in a five-week period later in the year. In the following 21 months, juries throughout the state imposed only two death sentences. Homicide rates, among the highest in the nation, hadn't changed. Observers suggested that jurors lost their nerve, now that a death sentence was no longer an illusion.

There are really only two political positions to take on the death penalty. You can support it or oppose it. The great irony about American capital punishment, as Zimring says, is that "no one on either side can defend the current system, which is hypocritical and unprincipled." Unless the purpose of the penalty is to create a gruesome illusion, there are just two alternatives. Those who write the statutes can narrow the category of killers eligible for death down to a manageable few, as many advocates of capital punishment are beginning to suggest. Single out the terrorists, mass murderers and contract killers. Use limited resources and political capital to maneuver them into the death chambers. After all, they're the ones—not the liquor-store holdup guy who panicked—that most citizens want dead anyway.

The other choice, of course, is to summon up the political will to commence executions in record numbers—at the very least, more than the nationwide high-water mark of 199 in 1935. That means devoting millions of tax dollars for more prosecutors, and new U.S. Supreme Court policy to give those prosecutors more leeway. In turn, that would mean more tolerance of imperfect justice. "I tell folks that if they want appeals limited to two or three years, some time we'll execute the wrong person," says Georgia Attorney General Michael Bowers. "Of course we will. We're human. But it's a question of will."

Which brings us back to Judge Kozinski, who kindled much of the current debate with his scathing indictment of the modern capital-punishment charade. Kozinski was appointed by President Reagan. Though a judicial independent and freethinker, Kozinski is firmly rooted in the tradition of judging that tries to keep one's personal views out of the courtroom. At times, he's excoriated his colleagues on the Ninth Circuit for not getting on with the death penalty. How would Kozinski feel about a system that produced several hundred executions a year?

"I'd hope it wouldn't affect how I handled cases, but I just don't know," he says. "I just don't know."

WHY AMERICANS APPROVE OF THE DEATH PENALTY

Christopher Hitchens

Christopher Hitchens criticizes the increase in American support for the death penalty in the following essay. Americans want to feel safe, Hitchens writes, and supporting the death penalty helps assuage their fears of violence. However, he points out, there is a minority of Americans who have rejected the death penalty as both a moral and legal failure, especially because it seems to be administered in an arbitrary manner. He suggests that support for the death penalty may decline should it be administered more often and to those from higher levels of the economic ladder. Hitchens is a frequent contributor to the *Nation* and *Vanity Fair*.

The American culture contains at least one enormous and self-evident contradiction, and American politics and institutions reflect this contradiction in very bizarre ways. The contradiction is more easily quoted than stated, because it is not a contradiction of which its exemplars are very perfectly aware. Coming right down to it then, the very person who sits next to you on that United Airlines long haul, and who sings high about how 'this is the greatest country God made' and 'the freest society on God's earth' and (lapsing into secular patriotic vernacular) 'the land of the free and the home of the brave', will most likely warn you, a few free drinks and a few mileage-club miles later, that it is nowhere safe to walk the streets, that old people are afraid to leave their homes, that children are in constant peril of every kind of sordid molestation and that only ruin and bankruptcy await the bold entrepreneur.

Forcing one to notice the same paradox in a different way, the more ideological types will say that state power needs to be rolled back, and that 'big government' is the enemy of the American ideal, and add that it's high time that the Supreme Court mandated the death penalty. I know a number of honest libertarians who refuse on principle to grant the state the right of life and death over the citizen, but even they make this point as if admitting that there is an 'irony'

This article is taken, with permission, from "Why Americans Like the Penalty of Death," by Christopher Hitchens, *Index on Censorship*, vol. 24, no. 2, March/April 1995. For more information contact, Tel +44 (207) 278-2313, Fax +44 (207) 278-1878, Email: contact@indexoncensorship.org, or visit Index on the Web at www.indexoncensorship.org.

involved: in other words, that rugged American individualists gener-ally demand that the state be more interventionist on this front. The point was nicely caught by a note in the *New York Times,* following the defeat of Mario Cuomo as New York's governor: 'Eleven days after he took office, George Pataki, New York's pro–death penalty governor, sent Thomas Grasso, a pro–death penalty murderer, back to Okla-homa to await death by lethal injection.'

In America, capital punishment is *so* popular that even the denizens of death row support it! Mr. Grasso had indeed demanded to be returned to a death penalty state for execution, and not long ago a child-slayer described in court as a 'calcified sadist' begged to be despatched by the notoriously auto-erotic means of strangulation. His wishes, too, were met, even though meeting them involved a change in the state laws governing execution. Not even this pornographic satire on the law was enough to stir any queasy afterthoughts. Pop-ulism rules and what populism wants, populism gets.

Americans Want to Feel Safe

With the exception of Japan, no other advanced industrial country executes people any more, but then no other 'advanced industrial country' is so close to the memory of frontier justice. No other similar society is so riven by ethnic and social rivalry. No other comparable nation has such a lurid gun-club following, or such an intimate acquaintance with domestic and civil homicide. So, at least the argu-ments run, often from both supporters and opponents. Yet in the past generations, Europe has been far more soaked in violence and revenge-killings, and the frontier ethic is not unknown in Ireland or Greece or Italy or Spain. Many other countries have horrid and intractable tribal quarrels, or civil-war memories. As for the violent crime business, it is true that America lives a crime drama on its screens and in its fiction and fantasy, and has exported the genre worldwide, but it is even more a fact that violent crime is falling by every useful measurement. (In New York, homicide rates have halved in the tenure of the present attorney general.) This is for the simple and intelligible reason that violent crime correlates raggedly, if at all, with other variables such as race, poverty, immigration or social dislocation such as unemploy-ment. It does, however, correlate very closely with testosterone levels; in other words, with the delinquency of young men in packs. And in America, the average age is rising, so that violent crimes per head are in decline.

This, perhaps, is to be too calculating. The violent crimes that do occur and are reported, are often of a peculiar heinousness that would exhaust the outrage deserved by many more crimes commit-ted in more banal ways. In a very rich, secure and highly-policed country, millions of citizens just do not *feel* safe. And their fear must be assuaged. It is not easily assuaged by a Constitution that appears to safeguard the rights of the defendant, that allows horse-and-cart loopholes to clever defence lawyers, and which prohibits 'cruel and unusual punishment'—the only form of words under which the penalty of death has so far been legally contestable in the Supreme Court.

A Chaotic and Arbitrary System

There is, however, a small but significant group of Americans that remains, or has become, convinced that the death penalty is a moral and legal failure. This group is drawn from the ranks of those who have to administer it. The former chief executioner at San Quentin prison, who was personally responsible for the largest number of despatchings in American history, wrote that it had had no discernible or measurable influence on the murder rate, and that it was in any case 'a privilege of the poor'. In an interview with David von Drehle of the *Washington Post*, Ray Marky of the Florida attorney general's office said the following: 'If we had deliberately set out to create a chaotic system, we couldn't have come up with anything worse. It's a merry-go-round; it's ridiculous; it's so clogged-up only an arbitrary few ever get it. I don't get any damn pleasure out of the death penalty and I never have. And frankly, if they abolished it tomorrow, I'd go get drunk in celebration.'

Ray Marky's testimony is significant because Florida has been the pace-setting state in executing convicts ever since the Supreme Court threw the issue back to state governments in the early 1970s. Governor Bob Martinez signed 139 death warrants in four years (sometimes, like [President] Bill Clinton, [former governor] of Arkansas, timing clusters of executions for tightly-contested electoral dramas). 'Old Sparky', as Florida's electric chair is obscenely or as some like to phrase it 'affectionately' known, has been in regular and continuous employment. But Florida's reputation for violent crime remains no less deserved and, perhaps equally important, the feeding of death row prisoners to 'Old Sparky' appears to be determined by some kind of lottery. Thomas Knight, for example, has been on death row in Florida for *20 years*. It took 10 years to incinerate the fabled serial killer Ted Bundy. Other prisoners, many of whom have committed crimes much less atrocious, are executed with relative speed. Nobody will be startled to hear that these have a tendency to be poor, to be non-white, and to be under-represented by counsel.

It is the latter point which has 'got to' Ray Marky. In an average case, if a defendant *can* get hold of a lawyer, the chances of getting a stay of execution, a judicial review of the sentence or even a fresh trial are so high that all possibility of consistency in the application of the supreme penalty has been lost. This would be true even if it were a penalty imposed at the federal level. But the mishmash of conflicting statutes operating state by state (such that Governor Pataki has literally to 'extradite' a man who says he wishes to be hanged in Oklahoma) makes an already anomalous situation into an anomaly in itself.

The "Other" Factor

'People think of capital punishment as something that is applied to "the other,"' says Leslie Abramson. Now celebrated as the stunning reversal-of-fortune attorney in the case of the Menendez brothers, she began her career as California's most intransigent opponent of the gas chamber, and has saved countless defendants from the death penalty. 'They never think of it as something that could happen to one of their own.' Insofar as this can be tested as 'perception', it holds up quite well. Black voters, who are generally very tough on law and order questions, always evince revulsion against capital punishment when polled as a group. This is what is vulgarly called a 'race memory'—the gibbet and the chair as the ultimate sanction of racism and exploitation. Black Americans also form the majority of those (at least two dozen in the twentieth century, according to a survey by the *Stanford Law Review*) who were executed while guiltless of any crime.

But though it's obvious that the death penalty is historically connected to racism, it may be reductionist to explain its popular appeal purely in this fashion. There are many countries and societies where crude opinion considers the crime question to be a subset of the gypsy question, the immigrant question, the religious question and so forth, but where democratic politicians are not under overwhelming pressure to sanction a penalty that they know to be ineffective and barbarous. It may make more sense to see the high vote for the death penalty as a version of the longing for simplicity.

In a very large and diverse and geographically-extended society like the American, where widely separated communities are knit together largely by information, a crisp and certain 'message' of any kind is relatively rare. Congressional proceedings are very muddy and extremely protracted; international relations highly complex and arcane; the pace of news and salesmanship often bewildering; the school system a mystery to many parents. Encounters with the bureaucracy are thwarting and frustrating. Might it not be salutary—might it not be *nice*—to see a grisly malefactor, just for once, taken straight from the dock and put up against a wall? Might it not be *clarifying*, and a good example for the rising generation? I confess to having thought this a few times myself (especially at the time of the Watergate hearing and the Oliver North trial) and to have felt cheated by the blizzard of paperwork and obfuscation and 'the law's delay'. The thirst for justice in America is kept permanently unslaked by a corrupt legal system to which only the rich have real access, so populist resentment is not to be wondered at. One healthy consequence, if one may speak ironically, is that nobody ever bothers to put forward the old and discredited argument about capital punishment as a 'deterrent'. People are honest enough to state that they only desire it as a release; as a cathartic action of moral abhorrence and irreparable retribution. Well, at least that clears *that* up—though of course it's odd in a society which contains such an apparent plurality of believing Christians. (Confessing the failure of capital punishment as a legal weapon, New York's attorney general Robert Morgenthau wrote that the Lord had said 'vengeance is mine.' He probably had tactical reasons to confine himself to the Old Testament, though even that manages to contain the First Commandment.)

A Civil Religion

Yet the United States, which is constitutionally prohibited from establishing any state-sponsored religion, still has a civil one. And that civil religion is law. Lawyers are the moral and the fictional protagonists of society, supplying everything from the bestsellers to the TV series to the movies as well as the real-life confrontations. And it is the cunning and complexity of the law that robs public opinion of its prey. At least since the belated statute against lynching took effect in the early years of the twentieth century, local worthies have been cheated of the right to immediate justice. Even the most appalling felon, equipped with no more than a bored and court-appointed attorney, can play out his frayed string for a year or two, while his victims (or their surviving relatives) bite their knuckles.

A very sinister change is involved, then, in recent attempts to change the law governing execution. According to a decision of the new Clarence Thomas-type Supreme Court, a defendant on death row who has exculpatory evidence can still be put to death if he fails to present that evidence past a certain deadline. So the much-loved Hollywood trope, of the last-minute telegram from the governor to the prison, is also for the chop. (I once waited for an execution at the notorious Parchman Prison Farm in Mississippi, where, as it happens, the black man who was gassed was later proven innocent, but where even as he waited for death it was evident to the wardens that he had not had a fair trial or a decent lawyer. At Parchman, gassings were always scheduled for five minutes past the hour, because Chief Justice Earl Warren had once telephoned with a reprieve right on deadline and been told he was a few seconds too late.)

The new [Republican] majority in Congress also wants to shorten the appeals process as being too bureaucratic and too much subject to procrastination and lawyerly manoeuvring. With this change, I think, the popularity of capital punishment will face a much more serious test than it has faced for generations. Until now, it has derived its support in much the same way as other supposed 'deterrents'—namely, by being unused. As it spreads, with Supreme Court and congressional complicity, across the states, its installation is certain to prove a disappointment. And what is more, it will more and more manifest its contradictions. A vile murderer will cop a plea here; an incompetent one-time killer will get the chair there. Innocent people will infallibly be shot or given lethal injections. The cost of the death row system, which is much more than some people imagine, will become more apparent. Above all, and even with 'speeded-up' terminations (because the speeded-up ones will certainly be the ones that give trouble when investigated), there will be a cultural conflict between America's exaggerated respect for 'due process' and America's political need for a 'tough on crime' totem. Like Mr. Pataki's cynical prisoner Mr. Grasso, populists may learn to beware of what they demand, because they may just get it.

THE DEATH PENALTY AS A COMMUNAL RESPONSE TO EVIL

David Gelernter

David Gelernter is a professor of computer science at Yale University. His book *Drawing Life: Surviving the Unabomber* describes his ordeal after being seriously injured by a mail bomb sent by Theodore Kaczynski in 1993. In this essay, Gelernter questions why, under the current legal system, America executes some penitent murderers while sparing the lives of unremorseful ones such as Kaczynski. Americans' self-doubt concerning capital punishment has made it difficult to impose death sentences, he argues. However, the author maintains, the death penalty is intended to send the message that all murder is intolerable. Society should consider it an obligation to "declare that deliberate murder is absolutely evil" by enforcing the death penalty, he concludes.

No civilized nation ever takes the death penalty for granted; two recent cases force us to consider it yet again. A Texas woman, Karla Faye Tucker, murdered two people with a pickaxe, was said to have repented in prison, and was put to death. A Montana man, Theodore Kaczynski, murdered three people with mail bombs, did not repent, and struck a bargain with the Justice Department; he pleaded guilty and will not be executed. (He also attempted to murder others and succeeded in wounding some, myself included.) Why did we execute the penitent and spare the impenitent? However we answer this question, we surely have a duty to ask it.

And we ask it—I do, anyway—with a sinking feeling, because in modern America, moral upside-downness is a specialty of the house. To eliminate race prejudice we discriminate by race. We promote the cultural assimilation of immigrant children by denying them schooling in English. We throw honest citizens in jail for child abuse, relying on testimony so phony any child could see through it. Orgasm studies are okay in public high schools but the Ten Commandments are not. We make a point of admiring manly women and womanly men. None of which has anything to do with capital punishment directly, but it all obliges us to approach any question about morality in modern America in the larger context of this country's desperate confusion about elementary distinctions.

Murder Is Intolerable

Why execute murderers? To deter? To avenge? Supporters of the death penalty often give the first answer, opponents the second. But neither can be the whole truth. If our main goal were deterring crime, we would insist on public executions—which are not on the political agenda, and not an item that many Americans are interested in promoting. If our main goal were vengeance, we would allow the grieving parties to decide the murderer's fate; if the victim had no family or friends to feel vengeful on his behalf, we would call the whole thing off.

In fact, we execute murderers in order to make a communal proclamation: that murder is intolerable. A deliberate murderer embodies evil so terrible that it defiles the community. Thus the late social philosopher Robert Nisbet: "Until a catharsis has been effected through trial, through the finding of guilt and then punishment, the community is anxious, fearful, apprehensive, and above all, contaminated."

Individual citizens have a right and sometimes a duty to speak. A community has the right, too, and sometimes the duty. The community certifies births and deaths, creates marriages, educates children, fights invaders. In laws, deeds, and ceremonies it lays down the boundary lines of civilized life, lines that are constantly getting scuffed and needing renewal.

When a murder takes place, the community is obliged, whether it feels like it or not, to clear its throat and step up to the microphone. Every murder demands a communal response. Among possible responses, the death penalty is uniquely powerful because it is permanent and can never be retracted or overturned. An execution forces the community to assume forever the burden of moral certainty; it is a form of absolute speech that allows no waffling or equivocation. Deliberate murder, the community announces, is absolutely evil and absolutely intolerable, period.

Murder Is Not Someone Else's Problem

Of course, we could make the same point less emphatically if we wanted to—for example, by locking up murderers for life (as we sometimes do). The question then becomes: is the death penalty overdoing it? Should we make a less forceful proclamation instead?

The answer might be yes if we were a community in which murder was a shocking anomaly and thus in effect a solved problem. But we are not. Our big cities are full of murderers at large. "One can guesstimate," writes the criminologist and political scientist John J. DiIulio, Jr., "that we are nearing or may already have passed the day when 500,000 murderers, convicted and undetected, are living in American society."

DiIulio's statistics show an approach to murder so casual as to be depraved. We are reverting to a pre-civilized state of nature. Our natural bent in the face of murder is not to avenge the crime but to shrug it off, except in those rare cases when our own near and dear are involved. (And even then, it depends.)

This is an old story. Cain murders Abel and is brought in for questioning: where is Abel, your brother? The suspect's response: how should I know? "What *am* I, my brother's keeper?" It is one of the very first statements attributed to mankind in the Bible; voiced here by an interested party, it nonetheless expresses a powerful and universal inclination. Why mess in other people's problems? And murder is always, in the most immediate sense, someone else's problem, because the injured party is dead.

Murder in primitive societies called for a private settling of scores. The community as a whole stayed out of it. For murder to count, as it does in the Bible, as a crime not merely against one man but against the whole community and against God—that was a moral triumph that is still basic to our integrity, and that is never to be taken for granted. By executing murderers, the community reaffirms this moral understanding by restating the truth that absolute evil exists and must be punished.

The Opposition's Arguments

Granted (some people say), the death penalty is a communal proclamation; it is nevertheless an incoherent one. If our goal is to affirm that human life is more precious than anything else, how can we make such a declaration by destroying life?

But declaring that human life is more precious than anything else is not our goal in imposing the death penalty. Nor is the proposition true. The founding fathers pledged their lives (and fortunes and sacred honor) to the cause of freedom; Americans have traditionally believed that some things are more precious than life. ("Living in a sanitary age, we are getting so we place too high a value on human life—which rightfully must always come second to human ideas." Thus [stated] E.B. White in 1938, pondering the Munich pact ensuring "peace in our time" between the Western powers and Hitler.) The point of capital punishment is not to pronounce on life in general but on the crime of murder.

Which is not to say that the sanctity of human life does not enter the picture. Taking a life, says the Talmud (in the course of discussing Cain and Abel), is equivalent to destroying a whole world. The rabbis used this statement to make a double point: to tell us why murder is the gravest of crimes, and to warn against false testimony in a murder trial. But to believe in the sanctity of human life does not mean, and the Talmud does not say it means, that capital punishment is ruled out.

A newer objection grows out of the seemingly random way in which we apply capital punishment. The death penalty might be a reasonable communal proclamation in principle, some critics say, but it has become so garbled in practice that it has lost all significance and ought to be dropped. DiIulio writes that "the ratio of persons murdered to persons executed for murder from 1977 to 1996 was in the ballpark of 1,000 to 1"; the death penalty has become in his view "arbitrary and capricious," a "state lottery" that is "unjust both as a matter of Judeo-Christian ethics and as a matter of American citizenship."

We can grant that, on the whole, we are doing a disgracefully bad job of administering the death penalty. After all, we are divided and confused on the issue. The community at large is strongly in favor of capital punishment; the cultural elite is strongly against it. Our attempts to speak with assurance as a community come out sounding in consequence like a man who is fighting off a choke-hold as he talks. But a community as cavalier about murder as we are has no right to back down. That we are botching things does not entitle us to give up.

Opponents of capital punishment tend to describe it as a surrender to our emotions—to grief, rage, fear, blood lust. For most supporters of the death penalty, this is exactly false. Even when we resolve in principle to go ahead, we have to steel ourselves. Many of us would find it hard to kill a dog, much less a man. Endorsing capital punishment means not that we yield to our emotions but that we overcome them. (Immanuel Kant, the great advocate of the death penalty precisely on moral grounds, makes this point in his reply to the anti–capital-punishment reformer Cesare Beccaria—accusing Beccaria of being "moved by sympathetic sentimentality and an affectation of humanitarianism.") If we favor executing murderers it is not because we want to but because, however much we do *not* want to, we consider ourselves obliged to.

Many Americans, of course, no longer feel that obligation. The death penalty is hard for us as a community above all because of our moral evasiveness. For at least a generation, we have urged one another to switch off our moral faculties. "Don't be judgmental!" We have said it so many times, we are starting to believe it.

The Difference Between Insanity and Evil

The death penalty is a proclamation about absolute evil, but many of us are no longer sure that evil even exists. We define evil out of existence by calling it "illness"—a tendency Aldous Huxley anticipated in his novel *Brave New World* (1932) and Robert Nisbet wrote about in 1982: "America has lost the villain, the evil one, who has now become one of the sick, the disturbed. . . . America has lost the moral value of guilt, lost it to the sickroom."

Our refusal to look evil in the face is no casual notion; it is a powerful drive. Thus we have (for example) the terrorist Theodore Kaczynski, who planned and carried out a hugely complex campaign of violence with a clear goal in mind. It was the goal most terrorists have: to get famous and not die. He wanted public attention for his ideas about technology; he figured he could get it by attacking people with bombs.

He was right. His plan succeeded. It is hard to imagine a more compelling proof of mental competence than this planning and carrying out over decades of a complex, rational strategy. (Evil, yes; irrational, no; they are different things.) The man himself has said repeatedly that he is perfectly sane, knew what he was doing, and is proud of it.

To call such a man insane seems to me like deliberate perversity. But many people do. Some of them insist that his thoughts about technology constitute "delusions," though every terrorist holds strong beliefs that are wrong, and many nonterrorists do, too. Some insist that sending bombs through the mail is *ipso facto* proof of insanity—as if the 20th century had not taught us that there is no limit to the bestiality of which sane men are capable.

America's Cultural Elite

Where does this perversity come from? I said earlier that the community at large favors the death penalty, but intellectuals and the cultural elite tend to oppose it. This is not (I think) because they abhor killing more than other people do, but because the death penalty represents absolute speech from a position of moral certainty, and doubt is the black-lung disease of the intelligentsia—an occupational hazard now inflicted on the culture as a whole.

American intellectuals have long differed from the broader community—particularly on religion, crime and punishment, education, family, the sexes, race relations, American history, taxes and public spending, the size and scope of government, art, the environment, and the military. (Otherwise, I suppose, they and the public have been in perfect accord.) But not until the late 60's and 70's were intellectuals finally in a position to act on their convictions. Whereupon they attacked the community's moral certainties with the enthusiasm of guard dogs leaping at throats. The result is an American community smitten with the disease of intellectual doubt—or, in this case, self-doubt.

The failure of our schools is a consequence of our self-doubt, of our inability to tell children that learning is not fun and they are required to master certain topics whether they want to or not. The tortured history of modern American race relations grows out of our self-doubt: we passed a civil-rights act in 1964, then lost confidence immediately in our ability to make a race-blind society work; racial preferences codify our refusal to believe in our own good faith. During the late stages of the cold war, many Americans laughed at the idea that the American way was morally superior or the Soviet Union was an "evil empire"; some are still laughing. Within their own community and the American community at large, doubting intellectuals have taken refuge (as doubters often do) in bullying, to the point where many of us are now so uncomfortable at the prospect of confronting evil that we turn away and change the subject.

When to Forgive

Returning then to the penitent woman and the impenitent man: the Karla Faye Tucker case is the harder of the two. We are told that she repented of the vicious murders she committed. If that is true, we would still have had no business forgiving her, or forgiving any murderer. As Dennis Prager has written apropos this case, only the victim is entitled to forgive, and the victim is silent. But showing mercy to penitents is part of our religious tradition, and I cannot imagine renouncing it categorically.

Why was Cain not put to death, but condemned instead to wander the earth forever? Among the answers given by the rabbis in the Midrash is that he repented. The moral category of repentance is so important, they said, that it was created before the world itself. I would therefore consider myself morally obligated to think long and hard before executing a penitent. But a true penitent would have to have renounced (as Karla Faye Tucker did) all legal attempts to overturn the original conviction. If every legal avenue has been tried and has failed, the penitence window is closed. Of course, this still leaves the difficult problem of telling counterfeit penitence from the real thing, but everything associated with capital punishment is difficult.

As for Kaczynski, the prosecutors who accepted the murderer's plea-bargain say they got the best outcome they could, under the circumstances, and I believe them. But I also regard this failure to execute a cold-blooded impenitent terrorist murderer as a tragic abdication of moral responsibility. The tragedy lies in what, under our confused system, the prosecutors felt compelled to do. The community was called on to speak unambiguously. It flubbed its lines, shrugged its shoulders, and walked away.

Which brings me back to our moral condition as a community. I can describe our plight better in artistic than in philosophical terms. The most vivid illustrations I know of self-doubt and its consequences are the paintings and sculptures of Alberto Giacometti (who died in 1966). Giacometti was an artist of great integrity; he was consumed by intellectual and moral self-doubt, which he set down faithfully. His sculpted figures show elongated, shriveled human beings who seem corroded by acid, eaten-up to the bone, hurt and weakened past fragility nearly to death. They are painful to look at. And they are natural emblems of modern America. We ought to stick one on top of the Capitol and think it over.

In executing murderers, we declare that deliberate murder is absolutely evil and absolutely intolerable. This is a painfully difficult proclamation for a self-doubting community to make. But we dare not stop trying. Communities may exist in which capital punishment is no longer the necessary response to deliberate murder. America today is not one of them.

ENSURING JUSTICE WITH THE DEATH PENALTY

George E. Pataki

In the following article, George E. Pataki, the governor of New York, explains why he signed a law that reinstated the death penalty in his state. Pataki contends that the death penalty helps to ensure the application of laws by giving the government a means to provide justice for wrongs committed against its people. The death penalty is an effective deterrent of crime, Pataki asserts; it can save lives by sending the ultimate message that those who commit murder are unfit to live among the other members of society.

On March 7, 1995, I fulfilled a major campaign promise and signed legislation reinstating the death penalty in New York. For eighteen years, the Legislature—the people's voice—overwhelmingly supported capital punishment. For eighteen years, New Yorkers' demands were thwarted by gubernatorial veto.

Under this legislation, those who murder a police officer, a probation, parole, court or corrections officer, a judge, a witness or member of a witness' family are subject to the death penalty. Someone who murders while already serving life in prison or while escaping from prison, or who murders while committing other serious felonies also is eligible. Contract killers, serial murderers, those who torture their victims or those who have murdered before also can be sentenced to death.

In determining whether juries should impose the death penalty on anyone convicted of first degree murder, the bill expressly authorizes them to hear and consider additional evidence whenever the murder was committed as part of an act of terrorism or committed by someone with two or more prior serious felony convictions. This is an important step toward ensuring that the law is applied to criminals who commit crimes such as two-time convicted killer Thomas Grasso, the World Trade Center bombers, or Colin Ferguson of the Long Island Rail Road massacre. This law is balanced to safeguard defendants' rights while ensuring that the state of New York has a fully credible and enforceable death penalty statute.

Reprinted from "The Death Penalty Brings Justice," by George E. Pataki, *Corrections Today*, vol. 58, no. 5, August 1996. Reprinted with permission of the American Correctional Association, Lanham, MD.

Reflecting the Will of the People

The most important characteristic of government is the service and protection of its members from enemies, both foreign and domestic. In the United States, government is an instrument of the people. Therefore, legislation must reflect the will of those who entrust representatives to create the laws of society. In New York, the overwhelming majority of voters demanded the death penalty.

The relationship between a government and its people is referred to as a social contract. The notion of a social contract dates back to when our ancestors first started to live in groups, but became a formal political theory with Thomas Hobbes. The concept is simple. We relinquish a little bit of our autonomy in exchange for safety, security and a sense of community for the greater good. Hobbes proclaimed that, without this arrangement, life would be "poor, nasty, brutish and short."

As societies developed, governments were created, and the people in the United States created the government to enforce the rules they had established. These rules, or laws, protect us and give a sense of safety that allows us to be concerned with more than survival. Those who kill violate the most sacred of understandings that we as a society embrace. With this violation comes the legitimate demand on our government to provide justice for wrongs committed against us.

The death penalty is society's way of telling its members that when you commit a crime as horrendous as murder, you are not fit to live among us.

The Death Penalty Can Save Lives

The death penalty will not bring back the victims of violent crime, but I am confident that it will act as a deterrent of crime and it will save lives. Those who disagree only need to look to the account of the August 1977 riot at Eastern Correctional Facility, where correctional officers being held hostage overheard inmates deciding against executing the hostages because, at the time, it was a capital offense. The deterrent saved lives. Without the death penalty as a tool for jurists, a murderer can kill again without consequence.

Another flawed position held by death penalty opponents is that once a criminal is behind bars he or she no longer is a threat to society. Consider the case of Corey Jackson, an inmate who was serving a 25-years-to-life sentence for a 1994 homicide. On May 9, 1996, he was convicted of executing three teens, on a drug dealer's orders, and was sentenced to three more life sentences. While awaiting transfer to a state prison from the Brooklyn House of Detention, Jackson slashed a handyman at that facility, Robert Manning, in the face with a razor. The attack on Manning left him with 60 stitches and a permanent scar. Manning was lucky to escape with his life. What makes this case even more disturbing is the fact that Manning sat on the jury that found Jackson guilty of the teen murders, and after Jackson's savage attack on Robert Manning, he yelled "You thought I couldn't get you, but I got you." It is evident that Jackson has no regard for the rules of our society.

For too many years Americans have lived in fear of crime. This New York law alone won't stop crime, but it is an important step in the right direction. The citizens of New York have spoken loudly and clearly in their call for justice for those who commit the most serious of crimes by depriving other citizens of their lives. New Yorkers are convinced that the death penalty will deter these vicious crimes. I agree, and as their governor, I acted accordingly.

THE CASE AGAINST THE DEATH PENALTY

Eric M. Freedman

Eric M. Freedman is a professor at Hofstra University of Law in Hempstead, New York, where he teaches courses in constitutional law and the death penalty. In the following article, he counters a number of popular arguments presented by proponents of the death penalty. For example, Freeman argues that the death penalty does not reduce crime; in fact, it decreases public safety by diverting needed funds from measures that are more effective against crime. In addition, he maintains that the death penalty is arbitrary in its administration and that the execution of innocent defendants is inevitable.

On Sept. 1, 1995, New York rejoined the ranks of states imposing capital punishment. Although the first death sentence has yet to be imposed, an overwhelming factual record from around the country makes the consequence of this action easily predictable: New Yorkers will get less crime control than they had before.

Anyone whose public policy goals are to provide a criminal justice system that delivers swift, accurate, and evenhanded results—and to reduce the number of crimes that actually threaten most people in their daily lives—should be a death penalty opponent. The reason is simple: The death penalty not only is useless in itself, but counterproductive to achieving those goals. It wastes enormous resources—fiscal and moral—on a tiny handful of cases, to the detriment of measures that might have a significant impact in improving public safety.

The Facts About the Death Penalty

Those who believe the death penalty somehow is an emotionally satisfying response to horrific crimes should ask themselves whether they wish to adhere to that initial reaction in light of the well-documented facts:

Fact: The death penalty does not reduce crime. Capital punishment proponents sometimes assert that it simply is logical to think that the death penalty is a deterrent. Whether or not the idea is logical, it is

Reprinted from "The Case Against the Death Penalty," by Eric M. Freedman, *USA Today* magazine, vol. 125, no. 2622, March 1997. Copyright ©1997 by the Society for the Advancement of Education. Reprinted with permission from *USA Today* magazine.

not true, an example of the reality that many intuitively obvious propositions—*e.g.*, that a heavy ball will fall faster if dropped from the Leaning Tower of Pisa than a light one—are factually false.

People who commit capital murders generally do not engage in probability analysis concerning the likelihood of getting the death penalty if they are caught. They may be severely mentally disturbed people like Ted Bundy, who chose Florida for his final crimes *because* it had a death penalty.

Whether one chooses to obtain data from scholarly studies, the evidence of long-term experience, or accounts of knowledgeable individuals, he or she will search in vain for empirical support for the proposition that imposing the death penalty cuts the crime rate. Instead, that person will find:

• The question of the supposed deterrent effect of capital punishment is perhaps the single most studied issue in the social sciences. The results are as unanimous as scholarly studies can be in finding the death penalty not to be a deterrent.

• Eighteen of the 20 states with the highest murder rates have and use the death penalty. Of the nation's 20 big cities with the highest murder rates, 17 are in death penalty jurisdictions. Between 1975 and 1985, almost twice as many law enforcement officers were killed in death penalty states as in nondeath penalty states. Over nearly two decades, the neighboring states of Michigan, with no death penalty, and Indiana, which regularly imposes death sentences and carries out executions, have had virtually indistinguishable homicide rates.

• Myron Love, the presiding judge in Harris County, Tex. (which includes Houston), the county responsible for 10% of all executions in the entire country since 1976, admits that "We are not getting what I think we should be wanting and that is to deter crime. . . . In fact, the result is the opposite. We're having more violence, more crime."

The Cost of Capital Punishment

Fact: The death penalty is extraordinarily expensive. Contrary to popular intuition, a system with a death penalty is vastly more expensive than one where the maximum penalty is keeping murderers in prison for life. A 1982 New York study estimated the death penalty cost conservatively at three times that of life imprisonment, the ratio that Texas (with a system that is on the brink of collapse due to underfunding) has experienced. In Florida, each execution runs the state $3,200,000—six times the expense of life imprisonment. California has succeeded in executing just two defendants (one a volunteer) since 1976, but could save about $90,000,000 *per year* by abolishing the death penalty and re-sentencing all of its Death Row inmates to life.

In response, it often is proposed to reduce the costs by eliminating "all those endless appeals in death penalty cases." This is not a new idea. In recent years, numerous efforts have been made on the state and Federal levels to do precisely that. Their failure reflects some simple truths:

• Most of the extra costs of the death penalty are incurred prior to and at trial, not in postconviction proceedings. Trials are far more likely under a death penalty system (since there is so little incentive to plea-bargain). They have two separate phases (unlike other trials) and typically are preceded by special motions and extra jury selection questioning—steps that, if not taken before trial, most likely will result in the eventual reversal of the conviction.

• Much more investigation usually is done in capital cases, particularly by the prosecution. In New York, for instance, the office of the State Attorney General (which generally does not participate in local criminal prosecutions) is creating a new multi-lawyer unit to provide support to county district attorneys in capital cases.

• These expenses are incurred even though the outcome of most such trials is a sentence other than death and even though up to 50% of the death verdicts that are returned are reversed on the constitutionally required first appeal. Thus, the taxpayers foot the bill for all the extra costs of capital pretrial and trial proceedings and then must pay either for incarcerating the prisoner for life or the expenses of a retrial, which itself often leads to a life sentence. In short, even if all postconviction proceedings following the first appeal were abolished, the death penalty system still would be more expensive than the alternative.

The Opposite of Justice

In fact, the concept of making such an extreme change in the justice system enjoys virtually no support in any political quarter. The writ of *habeas corpus* to protect against illegal imprisonment is available to every defendant in any criminal case, whether he or she is charged with being a petty thief or looting an S&L. It justly is considered a cornerstone of the American system of civil liberties. To eliminate all those "endless appeals" either would require weakening the system for everyone or differentially with respect to death penalty cases.

Giving less due process in capital cases is the opposite of what common sense and elementary justice call for and eventually could lead to innocent people being executed. Since the rate of constitutional violations is far greater in capital cases than in others—capital defendants seeking Federal *habeas corpus* relief succeed some 40% of the time, compared to a success rate of less than five percent for noncapital defendants—the idea of providing less searching review in death penalty cases is perverse.

Considering that the vast majority of postconviction death penalty appeals arise from the inadequacies of appointed trial counsel, the most cost-effective and just way of decreasing the number of years devoted to capital proceedings, other than the best way—not enact-

ing the death penalty—would be to provide adequate funding to the
defense at the beginning of the process. Such a system, although
more expensive than one without capital punishment, at least would
result in some predictability. The innocent would be acquitted speed-
ily; the less culpable would be sentenced promptly to lesser punish-
ments; and the results of the trials of those defendants convicted and
sentenced to death ordinarily would be final.

Instead, as matters now stand, there is roughly a 70% chance that a
defendant sentenced to death eventually will succeed in getting the
outcome set aside. The fault for this situation—which is unacceptable
to the defense and prosecution bars alike—lies squarely with the
states. It is they that have created the endless appeals by attempting
to avoid the ineluctable monetary costs of death penalty systems and
to run them on the cheap by refusing to provide adequate funding for
defense counsel.

Paying the Price in Public Safety

Fact: The death penalty actually reduces public safety. The costs of the
death penalty go far beyond the tens of millions of dollars wasted in
the pursuit of a chimera. The reality is that, in a time of fixed or
declining budgets, those dollars are taken away from a range of programs that would be beneficial. For example:

• New York State, due to financial constraints, can not provide bul-
letproof vests for every peace officer—a project that, unlike the death
penalty, certainly would save law enforcement lives.

• According to FBI statistics, the rate at which murders are solved
has dropped to an all-time low. Yet, empirical studies consistently
demonstrate that, as with other crimes, the murder rate decreases as
the probability of detection increases. Putting money into investigative resources, rather than wasting it on the death penalty, could have
a significant effect on crime.

• Despite the large percentage of ordinary street crimes that are
narcotics-related, the states lack the funding to permit drug treatment
on demand. The result is that people who are motivated to cure their
own addictions are relegated to supporting themselves through crime,
while the money that could fund treatment programs is poured down
the death penalty drain.

Arbitrary and Inhumane

Fact: The death penalty is arbitrary in operation. Any reasonably consci-
entious supporter of the death penalty surely would agree with the
proposition that, before someone is executed by the state, he or she
first should receive the benefits of a judicial process that is as fair as
humanly possible.

However, the one thing that is clear about the death penalty system that actually exists—as opposed to the idealized one some capital

punishment proponents assume to exist—is that it does not provide a level of fairness which comes even close to equaling the gravity of the irreversible sanction being imposed. This failure of the system to function even reasonably well when it should be performing excellently breeds public cynicism as to how satisfactorily the system runs in ordinary, non-capital cases.

That reaction, although destructive, is understandable, because the factors that are significant in determining whether or not a particular defendant receives a death sentence have nothing at all to do with the seriousness of his or her crime. The key variables, rather, are:

• Racial discrimination in death-sentencing, which has been documented repeatedly. For instance, in the five-year period following their re-institution of the death penalty, the sentencing patterns in Georgia and Florida were as follows: when black kills white—Georgia, 20.1% (32 of 159 cases) and Florida, 13.7% (34 of 249); white kills white—Georgia, 5.7% (35 of 614) and Florida, 5.2% (80 of 1,547); white kills black—Georgia, 2.9% (one of 34) and Florida, 4.3% (three of 69); black kills black—Georgia, 0.8% (11 of 1,310) and Florida, 0.7% (three of 69).

Double Discrimination

A fair objection may be that these statistics are too stark because they fail to take into account other neutral variables—*e.g.,* the brutality of the crime and the number and age of the victims. Nevertheless, many subsequent studies, whose validity has been confirmed in a major analysis for Congress by the General Accounting Office, have addressed these issues. They uniformly have found that, even when all other factors are held constant, the races of the victim and defendant are critical variables in determining who is sentenced to death.

Thus, black citizens are the victim of double discrimination. From initial charging decisions to plea bargaining to jury sentencing, they are treated more harshly when they are defendants, but their lives are given less value when they are victims. Moreover, all-white or virtually all-white juries still are commonplace in many places.

One common reaction to this evidence is not to deny it, but to attempt to evade the facts by taking refuge in the assertion that any effective system for guarding against racial discrimination would mean the end of the death penalty. Such a statement is a powerful admission that governments are incapable of running racially neutral capital punishment systems. The response of any fair-minded person should be that, if such is the case, governments should not be running capital punishment systems.

• Income discrimination. Most capital defendants can not afford an attorney, so the court must appoint counsel. Every major study of this issue, including those of the Powell Commission appointed by Chief Justice William Rehnquist, the American Bar Association, the

Association of the Bar of the City of New York, and innumerable scholarly journals, has found that the quality of defense representation in capital murder trials generally is far lower than in felony cases.

The field is a highly specialized one, and since the states have failed to pay the amounts necessary to attract competent counsel, there is an overwhelming record of poor people being subjected to convictions and death sentences that equally or more culpable—but more affluent—defendants would not have suffered.

• Mental disability. Jurors are more likely to sentence to death people who seem different from themselves than individuals who seem similar to themselves. That is the reality underlying the stark fact that those with mental disabilities are sentenced to death at a rate far higher than can be justified by any neutral explanation. This reflects prejudice, pure and simple.

Executing the Innocent

Fact: Capital punishment inevitably will be inflicted on the innocent. It is ironic that, just as New York was reinstating the death penalty, it was in the midst of a convulsive scandal involving the widespread fabrication of evidence by the New York State Police that had led to scores of people—including some innocent ones—being convicted and sentenced to prison terms. Miscarriages of justice unquestionably will occur in any human system, but the death penalty presents two special problems in this regard:

• The arbitrary factors discussed above have an enormous negative impact on accuracy. In combination with the emotional atmosphere generally surrounding capital cases, they lead to a situation where the truth-finding process in capital cases is *less* reliable than in others. Indeed, a 1993 House of Representatives subcommittee report found 48 instances over the previous two decades in which innocent people had been sentenced to death.

• The stark reality is that death is final. A mistake can not be corrected if the defendant has been executed.

How often innocent people have been executed is difficult to quantify; once a defendant has been executed, few resources generally are devoted to the continued investigation of the case. Nonetheless, within the past few years, independent investigations by major news organizations have uncovered three cases, two in Florida and one in Mississippi, where people were put to death for crimes they did not commit. Over time, others doubtless will come to light (while still others will remain undiscovered), but it will be too late.

The fact that the system sometimes works—for those who are lucky enough to obtain somehow the legal and investigative resources or media attention necessary to vindicate their claims of innocence—does not mean that most innocent people on Death Row are equally fortunate. Moreover, many Death Row inmates who have been exonerated would have been executed if the legal system had moved more quickly, as would occur if, as those now in power in Congress have proposed, Federal *habeas corpus* is eviscerated.

The death penalty is not just useless—it is positively harmful and diverts resources from genuine crime control measures. Arbitrarily selecting out for execution not the worst criminals, but a racially determined handful of the poorest, most badly represented, least mentally healthy, and unluckiest defendants—some of whom are innocent—breeds cynicism about the entire criminal justice system.

Thus, the Criminal Justice Section of the New York State Bar Association—which includes prosecutors, judges, and defense attorneys—opposed re-institution of the death penalty because of "the enormous cost associated with such a measure, and the serious negative impact on the delivery of prosecution and defense services throughout the state that will result." Meanwhile, Chief Justice Dixon of the Louisiana Supreme Court put it starkly: "Capital punishment is destroying the system."

THE DEATH PENALTY IS ONLY ABOUT REVENGE

Carol Fennelly

In the following article, Carol Fennelly draws a comparison between human rights violations in foreign countries and the use of the death penalty in the United States. She argues that the death penalty constitutes nothing more than revenge and urges Americans to focus instead on rehabilitating criminals. Fennelly approaches the death penalty from a Christian viewpoint, explaining that the gospel's emphasis on forgiveness should lead Christians to work for the redemption of criminals. Furthermore, she writes, if the United States is to have any say in international human rights issues, the nation must first address its own need for revenge through the death penalty. Fennelly is a frequent contributor to *Sojourners*, a Christian periodical.

Recently the world looked on in horror as 22 Rwandans were executed for their roles in the African nation's 1994 massacres that killed at least 500,000. Even more disturbing to the international community was the dancing, clapping, and whooping of the nearly 10,000 onlookers who turned out for the spectacle. The United States was among the nations speaking out against the punishment.

That same week the U.N. Human Rights Commission issued a stinging report that called for the United States to suspend all executions, saying, "A significant degree of unfairness and arbitrariness in the administration of the death penalty . . . still prevails." The report rebukes the United States for executing people for crimes committed as juveniles and people who are mentally retarded. It also found that race and economics play a major role in determining the severity of sentences. Religious leaders and human rights activists who have long called for doing away with capital punishment hailed the report.

In 1997, 74 executions were carried out in the United States. Consider this:

• Recently in Virginia the execution of a Paraguayan man was carried out in spite of the protests of the World Court, Secretary of State Madeleine Albright, and appeals from around the world. At the

Reprinted from "To Die For: The Death Penalty Is Nothing More than Revenge," by Carol Fennelly, *Sojourners*, vol. 27, no. 4, July/August 1998. Reprinted with permission from *Sojourners*, www.sojouners.com.

time of his arrest the man had been denied his right to counsel from his embassy.

• In an Arizona case, a Honduran man who had been denied similar rights was executed despite appeals from the president of Honduras.

• A Texas state legislator has introduced legislation that would make children as young as 11 death-penalty eligible. In Pontiac, Michigan, a 12-year-old boy is being tried as an adult for a murder he committed at age 11.

• In Denver, a local radio station called for listeners to drive by the station and honk if they wanted to "fry" Timothy McVeigh. Twenty-four thousand Coloradans did so. A *Detroit News* columnist hoped he'd catch fire in the chair, writing that "nothing smells better than a well-done mass murderer."

It was the highly publicized execution of Karla Faye Tucker in 1998, however, that finally put a sympathetic face to the issue of capital punishment and caused many Americans, including religious leaders who have been outspoken advocates of the death penalty, to raise their voices in protest. Tucker's evidently rehabilitated, redeemed, and repentant life illustrated to many for the first time that the death penalty is about nothing more than revenge.

Subsequent executions, including that of another woman, have been met for the most part with a ringing silence from many of those same religious leaders who were so outspoken over Tucker's death. However, for some Christians who traditionally have been supportive of the death penalty, difficult questions have persisted long after the issue left the front pages. For instance, the April 6, 1998, issue of *Christianity Today,* the flagship of mainstream evangelicalism, editorialized against capital punishment for the first time in its history. The *CT* editors wrote, "Jesus' teaching of non-resistance is difficult to live out on a societal level. Not all evangelicals agree on how to apply Jesus' teaching of non-resistance to public policy. But it seems clear that the gospel demands that in ministry, Christians work more for reconciliation than for retribution."

In a political climate that seldom plays to the noblest of our inclinations, "get tough on crime" is a much easier sell than redemption, reconciliation, and rehabilitation. In fact, 84 percent of Americans favor the death penalty under certain circumstances, according to a recent *Newsweek* poll.

Finding justice in the midst of evil can be difficult. Revenge is a much easier emotion to manage. The Catholic archbishop of Denver said recently, "The only true road to justice passes through mercy. Justice cannot be served by more violence." It is increasingly evident that the whole world is watching what we do on this question. Our moral capacity to speak to human rights issues internationally is compromised when we cannot quench our own blood thirst right here at home.

CHAPTER 3

THE ADMINISTRATION OF THE DEATH PENALTY

THE DEATH PENALTY CAN BE ADMINISTERED FAIRLY

John McAdams

Many opponents of the death penalty claim that it is administered unfairly; in particular, they maintain that black defendants receive death sentences far more often than whites. John McAdams takes issue with this claim, arguing that it is exaggerated and based on a misreading of statistics. Although he admits that the system is not perfect, he asserts that the death penalty is administered as fairly as other public policies and criminal sanctions. McAdams is an associate professor of political science at Marquette University in Milwaukee, Wisconsin.

We should, generically, want fairness in all areas of public policy. And we should especially want fairness with regard to the death penalty, since the stakes are high. But the opponents of the death penalty make a most peculiar argument about fairness. They argue that if the death penalty is not administered fairly, and especially administered with *racial* fairness, it must be abolished.

Nobody would even think of trying to apply this principle in a consistent way. If we find that black neighborhoods get less police protection than white neighborhoods, would we withdraw cops from both black and white neighborhoods? If banks are discriminating against black home buyers in mortgage lending, would we demand they stop all mortgage lending? If we find the IRS discriminating against middle-class and poor taxpayers, would we want to abolish the IRS? All right, that *does* have an attraction, but nobody is seriously suggesting it.

What do the opponents of the death penalty say should replace it? Life imprisonment, perhaps? But there is no reason to believe this penalty is more fairly imposed than the death penalty. So are we going to knock the maximum down to 10 years? If so, we face the same problem.

In addition to the philosophical incoherence of the argument, the empirical reality of racial disparity in capital punishment is a lot more complicated than simplistic notions about racism run riot in the crim-

Reprinted from "Can the Death Penalty Be Administered Fairly? Yes," by John McAdams, *Spectrum*, vol. 71, no. 1, Winter 1998. Copyright ©1998 by The Council of State Governments. Reprinted with permission from *Spectrum*.

inal justice system would lead you to believe. It's important here to understand that the opponents of the death penalty make two different arguments about racial fairness, and they are flatly contradictory.

Looking At Race

The first thing that we see when we start looking at statistics is that blacks are over represented on death row. Thus, we might conclude that the system is unfairly harsh on black defendants. Many have. As Frank Chapman said: "For 48 percent of the death row population in our country to be black is clearly practicing genocide when you consider that Afro-americans are only 12 percent of the population." Somewhat more recent figures show 41.7 percent of the death row population to be black, and of all prisoners executed since 1988, 38.7 percent have been black. Presumably, this is because of racist prejudice against black defendants on the part of prosecutors, or juries, or on the part of the voting public to which judges and prosecutors are responsible in a democracy.

I call this the mass market version of the racial disparity argument.

But then suppose we look a bit further. Notice that 48 percent of murder victims are black (in 1995). And then we notice that the vast majority of murders are *intra*racial and not *inter*racial. Among murders involving blacks and whites, 90 percent involve a white killing a white or a black killing a black. Almost three-quarters of the rest involve blacks murdering whites, and only a small handful involve whites murdering blacks. Knowing this, the number of blacks on death row, and the number of blacks executed doesn't look far out of line.

But we want to go beyond eyeballing numbers to get a solid assessment of bias. To do that, we have to control for factors that might legitimately result in more or less severe sentences. The opponents of the death penalty have actually cited the fact that blacks who murder whites are treated more harshly than blacks who murder blacks to argue for racial bias in the system. Unfortunately, the odds of black on white murders being comparable to black on black murders are about zero.

White on black murders are rare, and difficult to deal with statistically, so what we are basically left with is a comparison of the treatment of blacks who murder blacks, and whites who murder whites.

And what do we find when we make this comparison? As scholars such as Gary Kleck, William J. Bowers, Sheldon Ekland-Olson and David Baldus have shown, murderers of blacks who are themselves overwhelmingly black are treated more *leniently* than murderers of whites. Of course, this can be formulated in a politically correct manner, as a bias against black *victims*. As Randall L. Kennedy, describing David Baldus' study, remarked: In the marketplace of emotion, the lives of blacks simply count for less than the lives of whites.

I call this the specialist version of the racial disparity argument. I'm quite happy with this formulation, since it expresses concern for the victims of crime. But I can't avoid noticing that it flatly contradicts the mass market version.

The Racial Reality

But given that racial disparity is real, how severe is it? David Baldus, who is probably the top scholar in the area, recently described the statistical findings:

> . . . what do the data tell us about differences in discrimination in the pre- and post-Furman periods [after legislatures tightened sentencing procedures in response to the court's ruling]? There are significant differences in race effects, both across and within states. There are differences in the magnitude of race effects at different decision-making levels in the states i.e., prosecutorial decisions to seek the death penalty and jury decisions to impose death. There are also differences that correlate with culpability. The risk of race effects was very low in the most aggravated capital cases; however, in the *mid-range* cases, where the correct sentence was less clear; and the room for exercise of discretion much broader, the race disparities are much stronger. Whereas the overall average disparity for the two groups (black v. white) tends to be 6–8 percentage points, in the mid-range cases the disparities are typically two to three times that large [12 to 24 percentage points].

Baldus then goes on to describe some reactions to his findings:

> There is much anecdotal evidence from lawyers who represent capital defendants. Many of them seriously question the validity of statistical studies that do not reveal disparities based upon the race of the defendant. It is possible that there is such discrimination, but that it is not sufficiently large and systematic to be picked up by the data.

Baldus, perhaps out of politeness, doesn't note that lawyers are in the business of producing anecdotal evidence to support their client's position, and that those who represent capital defendants are a highly self-selected and hardly unbiased group.

As Fair as Possible

So what we have, in the way of hard statistical evidence, fails to support the politically correct fantasy of massive discrimination. Is the death penalty administered with perfect fairness? No. Is it administered as fairly as other public policies, and especially as fairly as other criminal sanctions? Yes.

Public officials should work to make the system even fairer. In particular, better provision could be made for an effective defense in capital cases. And I think that a revival of executive clemency (which has fallen into disuse) in cases where a jury is perceived to have been too harsh would be a good thing. But the notion that unfairness, and particularly racial unfairness, requires the end of the death penalty makes neither philosophical nor empirical sense.

THE DEATH PENALTY CANNOT BE ADMINISTERED FAIRLY

Leigh B. Bienen

In the following article, Leigh B. Bienen argues that the death penalty cannot be administered fairly because of ambiguous variables such as race that influence sentencing decisions in capital cases. Inconsistencies in administration also arise, the author explains, because certain crimes are considered capital offenses in some states but not in others. In addition, he contends, most jurors do not understand the provisions by which the Supreme Court enables juries to issue death sentences fairly. Bienen is a senior lecturer at Northwestern University School of Law in Evanston, Illinois.

Between 1976 and 1998, 38 states have re-enacted capital punishment statutes, and the state supreme courts have upheld those statutes. But from coast to coast, the death penalty remains fundamentally unfair and unjust. While unfairness in most policies is a cause for reform, when the stakes are life and death unfairness is cause for abolition. Capital punishment is unfair in its geographic variance; it is unfair because of its statutory ambiguity; it is unfair because of the extralegal variables, such as race, that influence decisions.

More than 3,000 people are on death row as of 1998 and more than 325 have been executed since 1976. Texas alone has executed more than 100 people.

Too Many Discrepancies

But a crime that is capital in one state may not be capital next door. The likelihood of being executed in Texas is far higher than in any other state. Just as a few miles can mean the difference between life and death, so can a few years. (California voters changed the composition of the California Supreme Court earlier in the 1990s by replacing three judges who were pilloried for overturning state death sentences. The remaining justices and their new colleagues now routinely uphold death sentences.)

Within a single state, differences in demographics or geography or

Reprinted from "Can the Death Penalty Be Administered Fairly? No," by Leigh B. Bienen, *Spectrum*, vol. 71, no. 1, Winter 1998. Copyright ©1998 by The Council of State Governments. Reprinted with permission from *Spectrum*.

prosecutors' policies cause huge discrepancies in the application of the same statute. For example, it is far more likely that a murder will be prosecuted capitally in a suburban or rural county than in a large urban jurisdiction. One county prosecutor will prosecute every death-eligible case capitally. In the county across the line, the prosecutor may plead out all but the most egregious murders, or choose to prosecute none as capital cases.

If vast differences exist between individual counties within the same state, larger differences exist among the states. Some states allow the execution of those under 18, a few do not. Many state laws allow those who do not do the killing themselves to be sentenced to death; others do not. Some states allow the execution of the mentally retarded, some do not. Each state defines the subset of capital murders differently, but in each state, the proportion of murders that could result in a death-penalty sentence is a fraction of all murders.

Each state supreme court interprets its own capital statute and the surrounding federal and state constitutional requirements differently. No one, not even capital punishment experts, understands the law.

Misunderstanding the Law

Jurors don't understand the law. Interviews with jurors show that they don't understand statutory aggravating and mitigating circumstances, the provisions that the U.S. Supreme Court said were to enable juries to decide fairly who would live and who would die. Jurors confuse statutory aggravating factors with mitigating factors because mitigating factors often sound like aggravating factors. Showing a juror that a candidate for the death penalty suffers from a mental disease or defect, or mental retardation or other behavioral deficits, may persuade some jurors that this is all the more reason to execute that person. And those are supposed to be mitigating factors, reasons not to sentence to death.

Jurors don't understand judges' instructions or jury selection procedures. More logical than lawyers, perhaps, jurors who are questioned at length about their attitudes towards the death penalty before a case starts assume that the death penalty is a possible, and perhaps even appropriate or expected outcome. Yet, jurors are not supposed to think about the death sentence until guilt is decided. Jurors don't understand whether they have final responsibility for imposing the death sentence, and if they do understand what they have done, they often assume the sentence will be reversed on appeal.

That judges don't understand the law is evidenced by the fact that there are so many reversals for extreme and embarrassing errors in capital cases. Judges worry about re-election and retention, and their pensions, and that they will be thrown out if they don't sentence to death. Prosecutors and defense attorneys don't understand the law, as can be seen in the reports of trials in the tiny fraction of cases that are appealed.

As a result of all this confusion, capital cases have a high rate of reversal. Almost half of all cases that came before federal courts on habeas petitions, when the federal courts considered capital cases on successive habeas petitions, resulted in the reversal of the death sentence. These death sentences were reversed reluctantly, not because federal judges were soft on crime, but because the errors and constitutional violations were glaring. Yet most state death sentences are not reversed, especially now that federal habeas has been restricted.

Certainly neither victims nor defendants understand the law. Anyone can understand how victims' families and loved ones would want the person who killed one of their own to die. In most cases theirs is the simplest and most dignified of responses, the easiest to understand. Nor is it difficult to see why victims' families end up angry and frustrated by the legal system.

The public and the press don't understand the law of capital punishment. How could they when gross factual and legal errors appear regularly in news reports? Lawyers who have studied the law and tried cases under capital statutes for years don't understand it. Statutory language and syntax are ambiguous and mired in confusion. The procedures for capital prosecution and trial are interpreted in a thousand different ways in a single jurisdiction, rightly or wrongly, and those decisions are rarely written down. Hence precedent, which is supposed to explain and iron out contradictions, doesn't exist. The interpretations of procedural statutes by courts, prosecutors and others are random and idiosyncratic when they are explained, partly because the participants in the process are angry and frustrated. All in the middle of it see an enormous waste of time, money and human resources.

Race, Class, and Other Factors

And as if all of these "legal" reasons were not enough, on top of everything else extralegal forces influence who is sentenced to death. Whether the case is newsworthy, where it occurs, whether the defendant and the victim and the circumstances have certain sympathy provoking characteristics, perhaps related to class, race and other nonlegal factors, will play a role in deciding who is charged with capital murder, who is prosecuted, who is sentenced to death and who is executed. The appearance of the defendant and the attractiveness of the victim may be more important than the aggravated nature of the homicide. And this doesn't even touch the subject of the role and influence of the media in capital cases.

Capital punishment clogs up the courts and wastes energy that could be better spent locking up murderers and making sure that the culpable are not released. Since so few sentenced to death are actually executed, less than one in 10, the system ties itself in knots and defendants end up sentenced to life anyway. So why not just sentence murderers to life, and forget about the circus of a capital trial?

Finally, though, it is a question of justice. Even if the present system were not a national embarrassment, even if it were not a waste of time and money, even if it were not irrational in the extreme, even if it did not corrupt and distort our system of laws, the reason to abolish the death penalty that overrides all other reasons is simple: it is not just.

Racial Discrimination and the Administration of the Death Penalty

Stanley Rothman and Stephen Powers

Stanley Rothman is the director of the Center for the Study of Social and Political Change at Smith College in Northampton, Massachusetts; Stephen Powers is a research assistant at the center. In the following essay, Rothman and Powers discuss the proposed Racial Justice Act of 1994, which was designed to prohibit the imposition or execution of the death penalty in a racially discriminatory pattern. The authors maintain that claims of discrimination in death penalty administration are largely unsubstantiated and based on faulty studies. They conclude that racial discrimination has nearly been eliminated from the capital punishment system.

On March 17, 1994, the House Judiciary Committee voted to incorporate the Racial Justice Act into the 1994 Omnibus Crime Control Bill. The Act essentially would create quotas for the administration of the death penalty, under the assumption that the penalty is applied in a manner discriminatory to black Americans. While the legislation has been opposed by House Republicans, one should not, given the temper of the times and the mood of Congress, discount the possibility that it eventually will become law. [Editor's note: The provision including the Racial Justice Act was struck from the crime bill by the U.S. Senate.]

The Racial Justice Act would prohibit "the imposition or execution of the death penalty in a racially discriminatory pattern." Further, the Act provides that to establish a prima facie showing of discrimination:

> it shall suffice that death sentences are being imposed or executed . . . upon persons of one race with a frequency that is disproportionate to their representation among the numbers of persons arrested for, charged with, or convicted of, death-eligible crimes. . . .

Excerpted from "Execution by Quota?" by Stanley Rothman and Stephen Powers, *The Public Interest,* no. 116, Summer 1994. Reprinted with permission from *The Public Interest.*

The Controversy

The employment of the death penalty as the ultimate criminal sanction has been the subject of enormous debate. Execution has been challenged not only on moral and religious grounds, but more recently on constitutional grounds—as a violation of the Eighth Amendment's protection against cruel and unusual punishment. Opponents of the death penalty contend that it is employed so arbitrarily as to amount to a game of state-sponsored Russian roulette. While the Supreme Court has not ruled capital punishment to be unconstitutional, in 1972 it held that the death penalty was unconstitutional as then practiced, finding evidence of arbitrariness sufficient to require that states overhaul death sentencing procedures.

One of the most controversial aspects of the arbitrariness claim is the charge—leveled by numerous activists and social scientists—that the death penalty has been applied in a manner unfair to blacks. In *Furman vs. Georgia* (1972), several members of the Court observed that racial discrimination had produced different patterns of sentencing and rates of execution for blacks and whites. Indeed, numerous studies of the late 1800s and early 1900s have found that blacks were executed in disproportionate numbers, particularly when the victims of their crimes were white.

The apparently discriminatory impact of capital punishment has not gone unnoticed in Congress. In fact, one aim of the Racial Justice Act is to circumvent prior federal court decisions which have held that statistical research does not provide sufficient evidence of "discriminatory intent" to trigger Fourteenth Amendment protection. The Act states that "it shall not be necessary to show discriminatory motive, intent, or purpose on the part of any individual or institution."

If the Racial Justice Act becomes law, state and federal authorities will have to demonstrate that any racial disparities in sentencing are "clearly and convincingly" explained by non-racial factors. Given the high cost of litigation and likely delays, as well as the difficulty of proving non-discrimination when sentencing is based partly on factors not easily subjected to statistical analysis (how does one quantify the "heinousness" of a crime?), states could be forced to abandon death sentences against some black defendants, irrespective of the merits of the cases. If this occurred, sooner or later it might also be an easy matter for white defendants to show discriminatory sentencing under the same law. The death penalty would be effectively eliminated.

But is death sentencing truly discriminatory? The truth is complicated by a number of factors that opponents of the death penalty have tended to discount or ignore. There appear to be legitimate reasons for racially disparate sentencing. Indeed, a number of social scientists have argued that racial prejudice is not a significant determinant of execution rates. These social scientists have demonstrated that when a number of legal factors are taken into account, the relationship between a defendant's race and the likelihood of execution tends to disappear. Why, we must ask, in spite of the questionable validity of the discrimination thesis, does the death penalty continue to be assailed as one of the most repugnant manifestations of American racism?

Past Studies

Before the Supreme Court's decision in *Furman*, a majority of death penalty studies had reported that discrimination against black defendants was substantial, particularly in cases of rape and in the South. Certainly there was ample historical precedent. By law, black slaves were subject to the death penalty for numerous crimes for which whites received much more lenient sentences. In 1848, for example, Virginia enacted a statute which required that blacks be executed for any crime for which whites might receive three years' imprisonment. The evidence for discriminatory death sentencing through the nineteenth and early twentieth centuries, particularly in the South, seems incontrovertible.

Even when discriminatory sentencing was not actually prescribed by law, statistical studies show that before the 1950s black offenders were much more likely than whites to be executed for murder. In 1930, H.C. Brearley reported that in South Carolina, from 1920 to 1926, blacks accused of murder were twice as likely as whites to be convicted. And during the period from 1915 to 1927, blacks were more than three times as likely as whites to be executed. Numerous researchers reported similar findings from the 1930s through the late 1960s.

Nevertheless, by the mid-1970s studies were uncovering methodological problems with some of the earlier research. In 1974, John Hagan reanalyzed a number of studies involving capital sentencing and found that most of the studies had confused correlation and causation. When Hagan controlled for prior record and type of offense, he found that the influence of race dropped dramatically. He concluded that:

> knowing the race of the offender . . . increases the accuracy of predicting judicial disposition by 1.5 percent. The causal importance of even this minimum relationship, however, is called into doubt by the single study controlling simultaneously for charge, and related "third" variables.

In a similar vein, a 1981 study by Gary Kleck found that between 1929 and 1966 the rate of execution for blacks (9.7 per 1,000 murders) was slightly lower than that for whites (10.4 per 1,000 murders). Indeed, Kleck made another important observation: "in the recent past, outside of the South, white execution risk has been substantially higher than the nonwhite risk, a fact which apparently has gone unnoticed in the literature."

In the past, Kleck suggested, black criminals may have been treated relatively leniently because their crimes against other blacks were not taken seriously, or perhaps because of white paternalism (blacks frequently were viewed as less culpable for their actions). In more recent times, Kleck suggested, the relatively lenient treatment of blacks may be due to the attempts of judges to compensate for what they perceive as institutional racism, or to make up for their own unconscious racism. Kleck also noted that his own figures do not take into account prior sentencing records and that, since in other studies this factor has tended to suppress racial disparities, his own findings probably understate the higher execution risk for whites. Overall, although Kleck found evidence of discrimination in certain historical periods (especially in the South), and for particular classes of crime such as rape, he found no evidence of system-wide discrimination in the imposition of the death penalty beyond the 1950s.

Since the publication of Kleck's study, many other studies have appeared that also find white defendants to be at greater risk in murder cases than black defendants, even in the South, though one or two of the studies have attempted to explain the findings away. . . .

Sentencing Blacks Who Kill Whites

With some research indicating that discriminatory sentencing of black offenders was confined to the South and probably had ended by the 1950s, sociologists began to search for more subtle evidence of discrimination. As far back as the 1930s, a handful of studies had reported that blacks who killed whites were more likely to receive the death penalty than blacks who killed other blacks, or than whites who killed members of either race. One of the first of these studies, authored by Guy Johnson, hypothesized that, as a subjugated race, blacks were "treated with undue severity." The author of the study found that in a sample drawn from parts of three southern states, black offenders were significantly more likely to be executed when their victims were white than black. Only 64 percent of blacks sentenced to death for killing other blacks were executed, whereas 81 percent of blacks who killed whites were put to death.

The researcher argued that blacks who killed other blacks were treated leniently because they were viewed by authorities as childish and not fully culpable for their actions. Yet when blacks killed members of the dominant racial caste, they were punished especially severely, to keep them in their place. Without considering the influence of factors other than race, the author concluded that the data "point toward a partial confirmation of our hypothesis." This failure to consider alternative explanations is characteristic of the research prior to the 1960s.

However, some later and better-constructed studies have reached similar conclusions. One study, published in 1983, found that the offender-victim racial combination was at least as significant a predictive factor in death sentencing as any other legal variable (e.g., contemporaneous felony, multiple victims).

A number of studies have attributed this seeming racism to prosecutorial discretion. A 1991 study in Kentucky, for example, suggested that prosecutors tend to view cases in which blacks kill whites as more serious than other types of cases. The researchers were cautious in attempting to explain why this might be, and pointed out that factors beyond the scope of their analysis might have been influential. Nevertheless, their study clearly implies that race continues to be a significant and obviously illegitimate factor in death sentencing.

Other Factors Must Be Noted

Still other studies have found that social class is an important factor. A few notable studies have shown that once one controls for the offender's social class, race becomes an insignificant predictor. For example, a 1969 study by Charles Judson and others found that race was not a statistically significant determinant of death sentencing. If anything, Judson's statistics suggest that whites were more likely to receive death sentences than blacks (48 percent of whites received death sentences, and 40 percent of blacks). But when Judson and his colleagues controlled for various crime-related variables, the influence of race disappeared. The socio-economic status of the offender, however, did seem to be important. Of course the substitution of one extra-legal variable for another does not justify differential sentencing, but it does suggest that our knowledge of the factors involved in sentencing is very limited. Indeed, the number of variables that can be shown to influence sentencing seems sometimes to be limited only by the ingenuity of the researchers involved.

A 1983 report of the Panel on Sentencing Research, commissioned by the prestigious National Research Council (NRC), concluded that even among the more sophisticated studies which found discrimination in cases with black offenders and white victims, race was a relatively weak predictive variable. The NRC panel cautioned that the "validity of statistical inferences about the determinants of sentences depends crucially on the methodological rigor with which the effects were estimated . . . [and] the findings presented here are weighed in light of potentially serious methodological flaws in research."

Other critics point out that key legal variables, such as prior record and seriousness of offense, have been difficult for researchers to document and even more difficult to quantify. Other legally relevant factors, such as degree of criminal intent, frequently have been overlooked. The fundamental problem with studies of the relationship between race and the death penalty is that they fail to establish convincing causal explanations. In fact, most studies demonstrate that numerous variables influence capital sentencing. For all we know, many other influential variables may be as yet untested. Some may be unquantifiable. On the basis of the available research, one simply cannot conclude that racial discrepancies are a function of racism.

Reviewing the history of research on race and sentencing generally, William Wilbanks found at least seven different "models of method and interpretation" in the literature. Despite the wide variation, he contends that some general observations on race and sentencing are possible. Among them, he includes the following:

> Racial discrimination in sentencing has declined over time. . . . The black/white variation in sentences is generally reduced to near zero when several legal variables are introduced as controls. . . . The race effect, even before controls, is not substantially significant, in that the predictive power of race is quite low. . . . Most sentencing studies have a large residual variation, suggesting that the models used did not fit the actual decision making of judges. . . .

These observations have proved to be especially applicable to research on discrimination and the death penalty. . . .

The McCleskey Case

One of the most effective challenges to the claim of racial discrimination actually arose in a court case that supporters of the discrimination thesis had hoped would prove their point. In the 1980s, the National Association for the Advancement of Colored People (NAACP) funded a major study of the effect of race on criminal sentencing. The study, directed by university professors David Baldus, Charles Pulaski, and C. George Woodworth, gained notoriety when it was used in the defense of Warren McCleskey, a black man sentenced to death for the shooting of a white police officer in Georgia. Defense attorneys relied on the Baldus study to substantiate their claim of systemic discrimination against black defendants. The study showed that in cases of mid-range aggravation [which refers to the aggravating conditions of the crime that are valid criteria in determining sentence severity], blacks who killed whites were more likely to receive the death penalty than whites who killed whites. (In cases of low and high aggravation, the study found race to be an insignificant factor.) The authors of the study argued that racial bias occurred because prosecutors and juries were prejudiced.

The attorneys prosecuting McCleskey countered by hiring an expert methodologist, Joseph Katz, who analyzed the NAACP study and found a number of conceptual and methodological problems. For one, it turned out that police reports often did not include some of the case circumstances that were supposed to have been weighted in the study. In these instances, the researchers recorded that the circumstances were not present, when, in fact, that was not possible to determine. Katz also pointed out that the researchers frequently weighted aggravating conditions in subjective ways. Most importantly, he argued that the researchers had not accounted satisfactorily for the fact that black offender–white victim homicides were often quite different from intra-racial homicides. Katz showed that black on white murders tended to be the most aggravated of all, and frequently were combined with armed robbery, as McCleskey's was. Katz also testified that by Baldus's own measures, McCleskey's was not a mid-range case but a highly aggravated one, and that in such cases the death penalty was as likely to be applied to whites as blacks.

The Supreme Court ended up rejecting the McCleskey defense, and ruled that statistical models alone do not provide sufficient evidence of discrimination. Later, Katz testified before the Senate Judiciary Committee, and offered further evidence of the differences between homicides in which blacks kill blacks and blacks kill whites. Katz reported that the reason why 11 percent of blacks who killed whites in Georgia received the death penalty—as opposed to only 1 percent of blacks who killed blacks—was that the killings of whites more often involved armed robbery (67 percent of the black on white cases, compared with only 7 percent of the black on black cases). In addition, black on white murders more frequently involved kidnapping and rape, mutilations, execution-style murders, tortures, and beatings. These are all aggravating circumstances that increase the likelihood of a death sentence.

By contrast, 73 percent of the black victim homicides were precipitated by a dispute or fight, circumstances viewed by the courts as mitigating. Katz also observed that 95 percent of black victim homicides were committed by black offenders, and that there were so few white on black cases that no distinctive homicide pattern could even be ascertained. Among the fewer than thirty Georgia cases identified by Katz as white on black, mitigating circumstances seemed to outweigh aggravating. These crimes rarely involved a contemporaneous felony and often were precipitated by a fight. This pattern may or may not hold outside of Georgia, but to date there has been no detailed national study of white on black crime. (Research has also shown that death sentences are especially likely in cases in which police officers are killed in the line of duty, and that 85 percent of police officers killed are white.)

Discrimination in Arrest Rates?

As pointed out earlier, some findings suggest that blacks may actually be treated more leniently than whites. Analysts at the Bureau of Justice Statistics have pointed out that the percentage of inmates on death row who are black (42 percent) is lower than the percentage of criminals charged with murder or non-negligent manslaughter who are black (48 percent). If the legal system still discriminates against blacks, why do they make up a higher percentage of those charged with murder than those executed for murder?

Some critics reply that the police may be more likely to arrest and charge blacks than whites. Yet we have found few data that support this assertion. In fact, Patrick Langan, a senior statistician at the Bureau of Justice Statistics, investigated the possibility of such discrimination and found little evidence of it. Langan based his research on victims' reports of the race of offenders, and found that blacks were sentenced at rates similar to those one would expect given the reports of victims. Obviously, this kind of research could not be conducted for murder cases (because the victims are dead) but the research suggests that the discriminatory arrest argument is highly problematic.

In the federal courts, the discrimination argument has found little support. In a number of cases, judges have concluded that the evidence of systemic bias is extremely weak. Rather than order an overhaul of the legal system on the basis of highly problematic and conflicting social science research, judges have preferred to adjudicate discriminatory sentencing claims on a case by case basis. The preferred corrective has been procedural reforms. A number of states have adopted clearer sentencing standards, various provisions to remove extra-legal influences, and the judicial review of death sentences. . . .

Politics and the Death Penalty

Clearly there are reasons other than statistical analysis for the continued belief that the legal system discriminates against black defendants. Those who oppose the death penalty on principle, for example, tend to incorporate the discrimination argument into their litany of protest. These critics perceive capital punishment as a vestige of an outmoded, barbaric, and irrational penal code. Black elites, meanwhile, often perceive discrimination in places others do not. They are joined by members of the white cultural establishment, who are quick to sympathize with those who allege racial unfairness.

This may sound like a harsh indictment, but how else are we to explain the facts? For decades, those who argued that the death penalty was administered in a biased manner maintained that the fact that more blacks were executed than whites revealed a lack of concern for black lives. When this argument became untenable—when it became clear that white murderers were actually more likely to be executed than black murderers—these same critics turned to other, equally unsatisfactory arguments. Now, however, they reject the implication of their previous view—that the execution of a larger percentage of whites than blacks must reveal a lack of concern for white lives. The only issue now is the race of the criminal's victim. These critics rationalize their position, but, we submit, their stance can be explained only by a need to find racism everywhere. One is reminded of the wolf in Aesop's fable. The wolf insisted that the lamb was injuring him, and was quick to change his story each time the lamb pointed out the factual errors in his claims. Finally, the wolf killed and ate the lamb anyway, proving that desire can overcome the failure of rationalization.

Questioning the Death Penalty on Other Grounds

If the controversy over racial discrimination and the death penalty turned on the merits of the research, politicians would have to concede that death penalty discrimination has been virtually eliminated. Alas, the news media have done little to clarify matters. Most reporting on the issue is inaccurate. An article that appeared in the *New York Times* on April 21, 1994, is typical. The article concluded as follows:

> That some bias occurs is not much at issue. Many studies show that juries mete out the death penalty to black and other minority defendants in a disproportionate number of murder cases, particularly when the victims are white and especially in states and counties that have a history of racial problems.

In fact, as we have shown, these comments are patently false.

Of course, many key questions remain. Is the death penalty arbitrary, given that only a fraction of those eligible are ever executed? Is it barbaric? Is it ineffective as a deterrent? If the answers to these questions are affirmative, two remedies are available: the death penalty can be abolished or subjected to further reform. But whatever society decides, such a decision should not be based on unsubstantiated charges of racial discrimination.

WOMEN ARE OFTEN UNFAIRLY SENTENCED TO DEATH

Whitney George

In the following article, author Whitney George provides a brief history of the execution of women in the United States. George concedes that compared to men, only a small number of women are executed, but she maintains that many women on death row were unfairly sentenced. For example, George writes, abused women who kill their abusers in self-defense frequently receive the death penalty. Race, class, and homophobia also play a role in determining the type of women who receive death sentences, the author concludes.

Maureen McDermott lives in a 6 by 12 foot cell 23 hours a day. She is allowed one hour of exercise each day on a small patch of black top. Three times a week she is taken out of her cell to shower. McDermott has been on death row since 1990 at the nation's largest women's prison, Frontera, in California. McDermott was sentenced to death for hiring a man to kill her roommate so that she could collect his insurance policy. She has fewer privileges, greater restrictions, and is more isolated than any man on death row in California. Maureen McDermott is a part of the small percentage of individuals who are overlooked amidst the legal and moral wrangling over the death penalty: the women on death row.

The battle between those for and against the death penalty has been heated since 1972 when in *Furman v. Georgia,* the United States Supreme Court ruled that the infliction of the death penalty was so biased that it qualified as cruel and unusual punishment. Four years later in *Gregg v. Georgia,* the Supreme Court sanctioned death penalty decisions under new reforms, and executions resumed the next year. Although the United States prison system has been plagued with criticism for police brutality, overcrowding, and inhumane conditions, Americans keep voting to implement the death penalty.

In U.S. history there have been numerous undocumented executions of women. Even before the first documented legal execution of a woman in 1632, women were persecuted for adultery, witchcraft, and

Reprinted from "Women on Death Row," by Whitney George, *Off Our Backs,* vol. 28, no. 1, January 1998. Reprinted with permission from *Off Our Backs.*

lesbianism. These persecutions of women are not mentioned in history books. This exemplifies the historical silence of women who have been killed by our patriarchial society. From the time of the witch hunts to the recent Supreme Court decisions, women have been condemned to death.

Between 1632 and 1997 according to Ohio University Dean Victor Streib, 514 women have been executed in the United States. This makes up only 2.7% of all people executed. In the twentieth century, 39 women have been legally executed. Despite the comparatively small number of women that have actually been executed by the state, women continue to be sentenced to death.

Between 1973 and 1996 there have been 114 women sentenced to death. During this time only one woman has been executed, Velma Barfield, on November 2, 1984. Sixty-six of the women's convictions were reversed or commuted to life in prison, leaving 47 women on death row in 1996. Many of these women have been locked on death row for over fifteen years and have exhausted their appeals. Will these women ultimately be put to death?

In the summer of 1996 Canada's Supreme Court reviewed 98 homicides involving women who are incarcerated, paroled, or have completed sentences they received for defending themselves against abusive partners. Justice Minister Anne McLellan and Solicitor General Andy Scott stated that two women will have their sentences reduced, two will receive conditioned pardons, and one will be entitled to a new trial. Canada, a country that does not have the death penalty, used Battered Woman's Syndrome as a defense to reexamine these cases. Battered Woman's Syndrome is an essential tool in reviewing cases where women have murdered men. "As long as one single battered woman who did not receive a fair trial remains in prison, the law has failed all who seek justice," writes Donna Jelenic, a victim of abuse from prison in Frontera, California.

Sixty-seven percent of the homicide victims of women on death row are men. Many of the male victims were killed by their female partner. There are a number of cases in which the women were prostitutes who murdered abusive clients or solicitors. Prostitutes enter the trial with diminished credibility and sympathy, which tends to lead to harsher sentencing despite their claim of self defense. . . .

Race, Class, and Homophobia

African American women make up 34% of women on death row, yet only comprise 6% of the total U.S. population. In 1990 the U.S. General Accounting Office reported "a pattern of evidence indicating racial disparities in charging, sentencing and imposition of the death penalty." One-half of all homicide victims are people of color, but 82% of all those put to death under the death penalty were convicted of murdering a white. This disproportion underscores the fact that the implementation of the death penalty is highly racist.

Poverty is also a factor when examining who is more frequently sentenced to death. According to Equal Justice USA, about 90% of those persons facing capital charges cannot afford their own attorney. Also, no state has met the standards developed by the American Bar Association for appointment, performance and compensation of counsel for indigent prisoners. Coupled with the racist aspects of the death penalty, if a woman is poor and kills a white person, she is likely to get extremely inadequate legal representation and therefore less able to defend herself against a death sentence.

As of early 1996, at least seventeen women on death row are lesbians, 37% of the total number of women on death row. This disproportionate number suggests homophobic discrimination within the justice system. "That so many lesbians are on death row and many more are being sentenced makes a clear statement about how the public feels about lesbians," says Robert Bray, public information director for the National Gay and Lesbian Task Force.

As portrayed in the hit movie *Basic Instinct,* the only thing more threatening to patriarchy than a woman who does not want men in her life is a "lesbian killer." One of the most publicized cases was that of Aileen "Lee" Wuornos, a lesbian and prostitute who murdered a man who solicited her for sex. Wuornos is accused in the murders of five other men. "Tell the women out there that I'm innocent. Tell them that men hate our guts. I was raped and I defended myself. It was self-defense. I could not stop hustling just because some asshole was going around Florida raping and killing women, I still had to hustle," said Wuornos in an interview with Phyliss Chesler.

Throughout the Wuornos trial, as in the cases of other lesbians convicted for killing men, the prosecution used lesbianism as a motive for the murders. "If we look at all the women on the row—not just the lesbians—what they've done is considered unfeminine," says Leigh Dingerson, executive director of the National Coalition to Abolish the Death Penalty. "For prosecutors, the worst crime is killing by women." The question arises whether these women are convicted because the media and prosecution sensationalize them as man-hating lesbians, or because they are guilty of the crime.

Abused Women Who Kill

According to the Women's International Network News, every nine seconds in the U.S. a man abuses his female intimate partner. Sexual, physical, and emotional abuse are often ignored by authorities when they occur within the home. This forces women to defend themselves or their children, sometimes by murdering their abusive partner. "Why did the system fail us? Why are we constantly asked, why didn't you leave? Why didn't the system make him leave?" asks Donna Jelenic, an imprisoned victim of such abuse.

It wasn't until the 1990s that the U.S. Supreme Court acknowledged Battered Woman's Syndrome as a legal defense for murder. Still today battered women who killed their abusive partner sit in jails and on death row. At the time many of these women were tried, the court did not permit their testimony of torment and abuse to be taken into account at their trials. "The juries were not aware of the vicious beatings, the rapes, the threats of harm and death and the extensive and ongoing emotional and mental battering [these women experienced]," writes Jelenic. "Two things that the patriarchy does to enslave women that are effective, one is isolation, and the other—silence. Between these two things, we are disconnected and we don't have access to our own power," writes Jelenic.

In the U.S. media, when a woman is convicted of murder, it is often portrayed as exceptionally shocking. When a mother kills her children, the public is outraged. Yet the fact that hundreds of women and children are abused and killed by men every day does not ignite the same firestorm and outrage. Women account for 13% of all arrests in the United States, yet they represent almost 44% of all murder victims. On the whole, women are by far less violent than men in our society. In fact, women are much more likely to be the victims of male violence rather than perpetrators of violence.

We are faced with a society that is largely informed by mainstream media that is influenced and owned by white upper-class men. In newspapers and television broadcasts, erasure of both women who are abused and women who are on death row is obvious. Since mainstream society has not acknowledged the horrors of violence against women and children, it is not a surprise that they also silence the women who kill to protect their own or their children's lives.

Women on Death Row Are Rarely Executed

Mark Hansen

In the following article, Mark Hansen explores the issue of sexism as it relates to the execution of female offenders on death row. In particular, he discusses the case of Guinevere Garcia, who was convicted to death for shooting her estranged husband in 1991. He notes that, as is the case with many women on death row, Garcia's sentence was commuted to life in prison during her appeals process. Hansen agrees with other commentators who contend that, at least in some cases, these commuted sentences can only be explained as evidence of leniency toward female offenders. Hansen is a reporter for the *ABA Journal*.

Guinevere Garcia should be dead by now. In fact, if she were a man, experts argue, she probably would be.

Garcia, 37, was convicted of shooting to death her estranged husband, George, while reportedly attempting to rob him in 1991. Hours before her scheduled execution, however, Garcia's life was spared, which is the outcome that awaits most women facing the death penalty.

Garcia's death sentence was commuted to life in prison without parole on Jan. 16, 1996, by Illinois Gov. Jim Edgar, who said that her crime was no worse than others that have resulted in lesser sentences. Edgar also said the decision to commute Garcia's sentence, his first in more than five years as governor, had nothing to do with gender.

Allegations of Sexism

Victor Streib, a law school professor at Cleveland State University, however, finds Edgar's claim hard to believe. Streib, who studies the issue of women and capital punishment, says gender is the reason women stand a much better chance of escaping execution than men.

"There's a sexism factor there," he says. "Fairly or not, we tend to screen out women as the process moves along."

While women make up about 13 percent of all murder arrests nationwide, they account for only about 2 percent of those who end up being convicted and sentenced to death, according to Streib.

Reprinted from "Dead Woman Walking: Commuted Death Sentence Raises Question Whether Females Are Treated More Leniently," by Mark Hansen, *ABA Journal*, vol. 82, April 1996. Reprinted by permission of *ABA Journal*.

Many of the women who do wind up on death row get off during the appeals process, Streib's research shows. Out of the 112 death sentences given to women since capital punishment was reinstated in 1973, 64 were reversed or commuted to life imprisonment. Including Garcia, only 47 of the approximately 3,050 people on death row at the end of 1995 were women.

Even so, women are rarely executed, Streib has found. Out of the 313 people put to death since 1973, in fact, only one was a woman.

The reasons for the disparity have a lot to do with the aggravating and mitigating circumstances that go into determining whether a convicted murderer gets a death sentence, according to Streib.

Women who murder, for instance, are not as likely as men to have killed in the past or to be viewed as premeditating the act.

Instead, women who kill generally are believed to be operating under extreme emotional distress or the domination of another person. And women who kill usually know their victim, which for some inexplicable reason is considered a less heinous crime than the murder of a stranger, Streib says.

Garcia's case in some ways is typical of the crimes that have landed other convicted murderers on death row. After all, she did kill her husband during the commission of another felony, which is one of the more common ways of qualifying for the death penalty.

And Garcia, unlike most women who kill, had killed before. In fact, only four months before she shot her husband, she had been released from prison after serving a 10-year sentence for suffocating her daughter in 1977.

But Garcia, unlike most death row inmates, had "volunteered" herself for execution, steadfastly refusing to appeal her sentence and eschewing all attempts by death penalty opponents to save her life.

Garcia's case certainly raises the issue of sexism in capital punishment, Streib says. And there are other cases that can only be explained by the fact that the accused was a woman. His research confirms what some in the field have long suspected.

A Historical Reluctance

Kica Matos, research director of the capital punishment project of the National Association for the Advancement of Colored People (NAACP) Legal Defense and Education Fund, says judges and juries in this country have always been reluctant to execute women. "It's just not done very often," she says.

Richard Dieter, director of the Death Penalty Information Center in Washington, D.C., says whatever bias may exist against executing females probably will disappear once a few more have been put to death.

And if the female equivalent of [serial killer] John Wayne Gacy comes along, Dieter says, he is convinced there would be no reluctance to see her executed. "The thing is, there aren't many women Gacys."

CHAPTER 4

THE INNOCENT ON DEATH ROW

Contemporary Issues
Companion

THE WRONG MEN ON DEATH ROW

Joseph P. Shapiro

Joseph P. Shapiro is a senior writer for *U.S. News and World Report*. In the following article, Shapiro discusses the issues surrounding the question of how innocent people can end up on death row. He notes that people who are falsely convicted are usually outsiders: members of minority groups, the mildly retarded, or those who are considered odd or unusual. Many defendants are coerced into making false confessions, he writes, and others are convicted on the basis of dubious testimony from fellow inmates. Shapiro also offers advice on how the system might avoid future wrongful convictions.

Gary Gauger's voice was flat when he called 911 to report finding his father in a pool of blood. Police arrived at the Illinois farmhouse Gauger shared with his parents and discovered that his mother was dead, too. The 40-year-old son, a quirky ex-hippie organic farmer, became a murder suspect. After all, someone had slashed Ruth and Morrie Gauger's throats just 30 feet from where Gary slept. There were no signs of a struggle or robbery. But what most bothered the cops was the son's reaction: He quietly tended to his tomato plants as they investigated. Eventually, Gauger was sentenced to die by lethal injection—until it became clear police had the wrong guy. His case is not unusual.

After years of debate, most Americans now believe the death penalty is an appropriate punishment for the most repulsive murders. But that support is rooted in an underlying assumption: that the right person is being executed. The most recent list by an antideath-penalty group shows that Gary Gauger is one of 74 men exonerated and freed from death row over the past 25 years—a figure so stark it's causing even some supporters of capital punishment to rethink whether the death penalty can work fairly. Among them is Gerald Kogan, who recently stepped down as chief justice of Florida's Supreme Court. "If one innocent person is executed along the way, then we can no longer justify capital punishment," he says.

For every 7 executions—486 since 1976—1 other prisoner on death row has been found innocent. And there's concern even more mistaken convictions will follow as record numbers of inmates fill death rows, pressure builds for speedy executions, and fewer attorneys defend prisoners facing execution. In November 1998, Gauger and scores of others mistakenly condemned gathered at Northwestern University School of Law in Chicago for the National Conference on Wrongful Convictions & the Death Penalty. They are "the flesh and blood mistakes of the death penalty," says Richard Dieter of the Death Penalty Information Center.

Executions have been rare since the death penalty was reinstated in 1976. But the pace is picking up. As of 1998, there are 3,517 prisoners on death row in the 38 capital-punishment states—an all-time high and a tripling since 1982. The 74 executions in 1997—the most since 1955—represented a 60 percent spike from the year before. Citing bad lawyering and mistaken convictions, in 1997 the American Bar Association called for a death-penalty moratorium. In November 1998, Illinois legislators voted on such a ban. That state, more than any other, grappled with the problem: It has exonerated almost as many men (nine) on death row as it has executed (11).

It's tempting to view the reprieved as proof that the legal system eventually corrects its mistakes. But only one of the nine men released in Illinois got out through normal appeals. Most have outsiders to thank. Northwestern University journalism professor David Protess and four of his students followed leads missed by police and defense attorneys to tie four other men to the rape and murders that put four innocent men in prison. "Without them, I'd be in the graveyard," says Dennis Williams, who spent 16 years on death row. "The system didn't do anything."

Most damning of the current system would be proof that a guiltless person has been executed. Credible, but not clear-cut, claims of innocence have been raised in a handful of executions since 1976. Leonel Herrera died by lethal injection in Texas in 1993 even though another man confessed to the murder. The U.S. Supreme Court ruled that, with his court appeals exhausted, an extraordinary amount of proof was required to stop his execution. Governors, the court noted, can still grant clemency in such cases. But what was once common is now so politically risky that only about one death row inmate a year wins such freedom.

How Wrongful Convictions Happen

Gary Gauger's calm gave a cop a hunch. But it was Gauger's trusting nature that gave police a murder tale that day in 1993. Gauger says that during 18 hours of nonstop interrogation, detectives insisted they had a "stack of evidence" against him. They didn't—but it never occurred to the laid-back farmer that his accusers might be lying. Instead, he worried he might have blacked out the way he sometimes did in the days when he drank heavily. So Gauger went along with police suggestions that, to jog his memory, he hypothetically describe the murders. After viewing photos of his mother's slit throat, Gauger explained how he could have walked into her rug shop next to the house ("she knows and trusts me"), pulled her hair, slashed her throat and then done the same to his dad as he worked in his nearby antique-motorcycle shop. To police, this was a chilling confession. Even Gauger, by this point suicidal, believed he must have committed the crimes.

Though police failed to turn up any physical evidence during a 10-day search of the farm, prosecutors depicted Gauger as an oddball who could have turned on his mother and father. He was a pot-smoking ex-alcoholic who once lived on a commune and brought his organic farming ways back to Richmond, Ill. The judge rolled his eyes during Gauger's testimony and, when defense attorneys objected, simply turned his back on Gauger. The jury took just three hours to reach a guilty verdict. "Nutty as a fruitcake," the jury foreman declared afterward.

A study by Profs. Hugo Bedau of Tufts University and Michael Radelet of the University of Florida found three factors common among wrongful capital convictions. One third involve perjured testimony, often from jailhouse snitches claiming to have heard a defendant's prison confession. (At Gauger's trial, a fellow inmate made a dubious claim to hearing Gauger confess. The man, contacted in jail by *U.S. News*, offered to tell a very different story if the magazine would pay for an interview.) One of every 7 cases, Bedau and Radelet found, involves faulty eyewitness identifications, and a seventh involve false confessions, like Gauger's.

False confessions occur with greater frequency than recognized even by law-enforcement professionals, argues Richard Leo of the University of California—Irvine. About a quarter, he estimates, involve people with mild mental retardation, who often try to hide limitations by guessing "right" answers to police questions. Children are vulnerable, too. Chicago police in September 1998 dropped murder charges against two boys, 7 and 8 years old, who confessed to killing 11-year-old Ryan Harris with a rock to steal her bicycle. After a crime laboratory found semen on the dead girl's clothes, police began looking for an older suspect. An educated innocent person, likely to trust police, may be especially prone to police trickery—which courts allow as often necessary to crack savvy criminals. "My parents had just been murdered and these were the good guys," Gauger says. "I know it sounds naive now, but when they told me they wouldn't lie to me, I believed them."

The falsely convicted is almost always an outsider—often from a minority group. In Illinois, six of the nine dismissed from death row were black or Hispanic men accused of murder, rape, or both of white victims. But the No. 1 reason people are falsely convicted is poor legal representation. Many states cap fees for court-appointed attorneys, which makes it tough for indigents to get competent lawyers. And it's been harder for inmates to find lawyers to handle appeals since Congress in 1996 stopped funding legal-aid centers in 20 states.

How Wrongful Convictions Get Discovered

Gary Gauger has a simple answer to how he won his freedom: "I got lucky." Of all the 74 released from death row, Gauger's stay was one of the briefest—just eight months. Shortly after his conviction, FBI agents listening in on a wiretap overheard members of a motorcycle gang discussing the murder of Ruth and Morrie Gauger. In 1997, two members of the Outlaws Motorcycle Club, Randall "Madman" Miller and James "Preacher" Schneider, were indicted for the Gauger killings. But in October 1998, a federal judge ruled the wiretaps were unauthorized and dismissed all the charges. The U.S. Attorney says he is seeking to reinstate them.

Even when another person confesses, the legal system can be slow to respond. Rolando Cruz and Alejandro Hernandez spent 10 years each on death row in Illinois for the rape and murder of 10-year-old Jeanine Nicarico. Shortly after their convictions, police arrested a repeat sex offender and murderer named Brian Dugan who confessed to the crime, providing minute details unknown to the public. Prosecutors still insisted Cruz and Hernandez were the killers—even after DNA testing linked Dugan to the crime. At Cruz's third trial, a police officer admitted that he'd lied when he testified Cruz had confessed in a "vision" about the girl's murder. The judge then declared Cruz not guilty. . . .

Discarded Evidence

DNA profiling, perhaps more than any other development, has exposed the fallibility of the legal system. In the last decade, 56 wrongfully convicted people have won release because of DNA testing, 10 of them from death row. Attorneys Barry Scheck and Peter Neufeld, with the help of their students at New York's Cardozo School of Law, have freed 35 of those. But their Innocence Project has been hobbled by the fact that, in 70 percent of the cases they pursued police had already discarded semen, hair, or other evidence needed for testing.

Gauger had one other thing going for him that is key to overturning bogus convictions: outside advocates. Most important was his twin sister, Ginger, who convinced Northwestern Law School Prof. Lawrence Marshall . . . to help her brother a week before the deadline for the final state appeal. In September 1994, Gauger's death sentence was reduced to life in prison. Two years later, he was freed. Marshall visited Gauger in prison with the surprise news. "That's good," he said with a smile and his customary calm.

How To Prevent Wrongful Convictions

It's a fall afternoon and starlings are fluttering through the colorful maples that frame the Gauger farmhouse. Gary Gauger loads a dusty pickup with pumpkins, squash, and other vegetables. Inside, Ginger has taken up her mother's business of selling Asian kilims and American Indian pottery. A friend runs the vintage-motorcycle business, still called Morrie's Place, in an adjoining garage. For Gary Gauger, life seems normal again. Customers at his vegetable stand sort through bushels of squash. A hand-lettered sign advises: "Self Service: please place money in black box . . . thanks."

But there is pain, too, for his lost parents and for his 3½ lost years. And it's that part of his story Gauger shared at the conference in the hope of sparing others such pain. Other conferees at the Northwestern event endorsed a moratorium on executions at least until safeguards are in place such as increased legal aid, certification of capital-trial attorneys, limits on use of jail-house snitches, access to post-conviction DNA testing, and the recording of all police interrogations. There were also appeals for accreditation of forensic experts: The first Cruz trial turned on a bloody footprint identified by an expert who was later discredited when she claimed she could tell a person's class and race by shoe imprints.

Gauger says the worst part about being wrongfully convicted is knowing that the guilty person is free. The victim Gauger most thinks about is 7-year-old Melissa Ackerman. The little girl was grabbed from her bicycle, sodomized, and left in an irrigation ditch, her body so unrecognizable that she could be identified only by dental records. She was killed by Brian Dugan, while Rolando Cruz and Alejandro Hernandez sat behind bars—falsely convicted of another child's murder committed by Dugan.

MISTAKEN EXECUTIONS CANNOT BE CORRECTED

Jonathan Rauch

Jonathan Rauch is a staff correspondent for the *National Journal* and the author of several books. Although he believes that the death penalty is just, Rauch writes, he is troubled about the possibility of executing the wrong person. Rauch specifically explores the case of Leo Alexander Jones, a known drug dealer who was convicted of killing a police officer even though the evidence strongly supported his claim of innocence. In addition, Rauch discusses the politics of death penalty cases in a time when leniency for capital crimes is harmful to governors' chances for reelection.

The corner of Sixth and Davis Streets in Jacksonville, Florida, is a kind of cemetery without graves. Nothing remains here but vacant lots and wild grass that ripples in Florida's gray spring wind. You have to use your imagination to see this place as it was in 1981, when there were shabby tenement houses, and a bar, and a store, and a great deal of violence. This was Jacksonville's teeming drug ghetto then, full of guns and fear that spilled over from the housing projects nearby. The police came here often.

The Death of a Policeman

At 1 A.M. in the early morning of May 23, 1981, three police cars drove in caravan to the stop sign at Sixth and Davis, all of them leaving the scene of a domestic disturbance. The first two turned left without incident. Then came two or three loud reports. A sniper's bullet pierced the windshield of the third car, struck metal inside and broke into fragments, which ricocheted into the driver's skull. The first policeman to reach the car found Officer Thomas J. Szafranski seized up against the steering wheel in unconscious convulsions, his hair and blood splattering the inside of the car. Szafranski died the next day. He was only 29.

Within minutes the place was swarming with cops. But where had the shot come from? Some people thought it came from a vacant lot across Davis Street, others pointed to a run-down duplex house and drug den just beside the vacant lot. One of the police officers driving ahead of Szafranski, on hearing the first shot, had turned quickly enough to see muzzle fire from the house as more shots were fired, lighting up the front porch like flash bulbs. Several officers stormed the house. Inside one of its four apartments they found Leo Alexander Jones, who was a 31-year-old drug dealer with two prior felony convictions, and his cousin, a man named Bobby Hammonds. The two resisted arrest and there was a violent scuffle, the police said. Under Jones's bed were two Winchester .30-.30 caliber Marlin rifles, each containing a single spent shell. One rifle had Jones's fingerprint on the breech. The bullet that had killed Szafranski was too badly damaged to be traced to any particular weapon. But it had come from a Winchester .30-.30 Marlin.

After several hours of police interrogation, Jones signed a confession written out by a detective. It said: "I, Leo Jones, on 23 May 81 took a rifle out of the front room of my apartment and went down the back stairs and walked to the front empty apartment and shot the policeman through the front window of the apartment. I then ran back upstairs and hid the gun or rifle and then the police came."

Death and Politics

In 1997, America executed 74 people. "This is the most executions in a single year since the 76 inmates executed in 1955," notes the federal Bureau of Justice Statistics. Judging from the rate through April, 1998's count will exceed 1997's. The death row population has tripled since 1982.

In the past 10 years, three states—New York, Kansas and New Hampshire—have added the death penalty; none has abolished it. In the 1994 crime bill, Congress created several dozen new death penalty crimes, including death for certain drug offenses. The courts have ruled that capital punishment is unconstitutionally harsh for crimes in which a life isn't taken, but that doesn't seem to be giving politicians much pause. In 1995, House Speaker Newt Gingrich of Georgia demanded death for drug smugglers, and suggested that mass executions, "27 or 30 or 35 people at one time," might make an excellent deterrent. Al Checchi, a Democrat in California, demands the death penalty for serial rapists and repeat child molesters, who, he says, "kill the spirit of a woman or a child."

Unfortunately, that is about as deep as the current political argument over the death penalty usually goes. Given that the power to kill is the most fearful and potent weapon the state possesses, it seems peculiar that Washington spends vastly more time and energy debating capital gains than capital punishment. It is also peculiar that people who do talk about the death penalty, whether they support or oppose it, pay so little attention to the question of wrongful execution, which goes to the very core of a liberal government's legitimacy.

The Trial Proceedings

At Jones's trial, the state made a compelling case. The shots had come from Jones's building, the prosecution's witnesses said. Bobby Hammonds testified that he saw Jones leave his apartment with a rifle, heard the gunshots, and then saw Jones return with the rifle. A police officer testified that, in a car-search incident a week earlier, Jones had said he was tired of being hassled by police and "he was going to shoot him a motherfucking pig." There was also the confession, and the rifle.

Jones denied threatening to kill a cop. The defense produced witnesses saying that the shots had come not from Jones's house but from the field beside it. And if there were two or three shots, where were the missing shells? The rifles, Jones maintained, belonged to a friend of his, one Glen Schofield. As for Bobby Hammonds, he kept changing his story. When the police interrogated him, he implicated Jones, but then, in a sworn statement, he recanted; at the trial, he implicated Jones again; after the trial, he recanted a second time, claiming police coercion. Jones, too, claimed coercion. He said the police had beaten the confession out of him, that he was half-senseless and in fear for his life when he initialed it.

Nonsense, said the state. Jones had been taken to the hospital after his arrest and was found to have only superficial injuries, from the scuffle. For the six hours before he confessed, he had not been touched, as he himself acknowledged. The jury returned the sentence of death by electrocution.

Death and Justice

Timothy McVeigh now waits on death row in a maximum-security federal prison in Florence, Colo. In the bombing of the Alfred P. Murrah Federal Building in Oklahoma City in 1995, 168 people died, all of them innocent and 19 of them children. Assuming McVeigh really did this thing, you can imagine two civilized responses. One says that society shows its esteem for life by refusing to kill. In that case, executing McVeigh would do nothing more than add a 169th body to the pile. The other response says that any punishment less severe than death mocks the value of those 168 lives. . . .

If you think that executing McVeigh, or anybody else, is unjust, then you know what you think about capital punishment. But if you believe, along with me and the American majority, that capital punishment is just, at least for heinous killers, you must still advance to the next question. What if we kill the wrong person?

The Evidence Points Elsewhere

"Where is Glen Schofield?" asked Jones's defense lawyer at the trial in 1981. It was a question that would be asked often. Schofield was a drug-dealing crony of Jones's, a violent man on parole for manslaughter. Some hours before the murder, he had turned up in Jones's apartment with a pistol. The police knew him all too well, and considered him a suspect. But they found no trace of him in the neighborhood at the time of the murder, and no evidence tying him to the crime.

Schofield had an alibi. In fact, he had a couple of them. In one, he was with one of his girlfriends on the night of the murder. (Apparently, no one checked this story with her.) Later, after the trial, he claimed to have been with a woman friend named "Marilyn Manning" and a man he knew only as "Shorty."

In 1984, Jones got a new and more energetic lawyer. The lawyer's investigator turned up Schofield's friend Marion Manning, and she said that on the night of the murder, not long after the shots were fired, Shorty had flagged her down and asked her to pick up Schofield, who told her to "get the hell out of here" because Jones had just shot a guy. Schofield admitted that he had been dancing with her that night, but he denied the rest.

During the 1980s, the Jones case dragged on in fits and starts through its various stages of appeal. Meanwhile, other things happened:

In the mid-1980s, the policeman who arrested Jones, and whom Jones accused of beating him, was forced out of uniform under an ethical cloud. So, separately, was one of the detectives who took Jones's confession. In 1985 came another tidbit. A state convict named Paul Marr, in prison with Schofield (who by then had landed in jail for various felonies), told Jones's lawyers that Schofield had boasted of the Jacksonville killing.

In 1991, yet another set of public defense lawyers took over Jones's case. A tip led them to Denise Reed and her boyfriend Daniel Cole, who both said that on the night of the murder, as they walked home from a movie, they saw Glen Schofield running from the direction of the crime with a rifle. Reed's mother confirmed that her daughter had told her the story that same night. Both of the young people said they had kept mum out of fear of Schofield and his friends.

Then the investigators checked with Schofield's (by-now-former) girlfriend, Patricia Owens Farrel, whom he had given as his original alibi. She told them Schofield was not with her that night, and that when she did see him he told her, "Pat, if anybody wants to know where I was, tell them I was with you."

Meanwhile, another in a series of death warrants was signed for Jones. This generated publicity, and now more prison inmates—three or four—came forward to report that Schofield had bragged of killing the cop in Jacksonville. One of them reported, "He said [Szafranski] kept hassling him on the streets about dealing drugs."

Armed with this new information, the defense received a stay of execution and a hearing on its motion to vacate Jones's conviction. The appeal ground on, and in 1996 the defense lost before the Florida

Supreme Court. Early in 1997, another warrant was signed for Jones's execution.

Death and Innocence

How many innocent people, if any, have been executed? One might imagine the answer would be nothing more complicated than a number: one, 10, 100; 1 per cent, 10 per cent. But there is no number.

We can figure your chances of dying on the highway, or getting cancer from cigarettes, because we know how many people drive and die in cars, and how many smoke and get cancer. But we can't say anything about the prevalence of wrongful execution without knowing whether any particular execution was wrongful. Unfortunately, the only way to decide whether an execution was wrongful is to examine the case carefully and decide whether justice was done. That, of course, is exactly what the original process tried to do, except that we must do it afterward, when the evidence is stale, the trail is cold and the defense's key witness lies in his grave.

In 1987, Hugo Adam Bedau, a philosopher at Tufts University, and Michael L. Radelet, a sociologist at the University of Florida, published a paper identifying what they said were 23 wrongful executions since 1905. Only one of those, however, was recent. In any case, the authors' method was mainly to examine the record, from which they concluded that the defense seemed right. They were immediately attacked by Stephen J. Markman and Paul G. Cassell, two officials in the Reagan Administration's Justice Department, who examined a dozen of the same 23 cases and concluded that each defendant was in fact guilty. Their method was also to examine the record, from which they concluded that the state was right. Both sides concede that nothing was resolved, and there has been no subsequent systematic research.

Cassell, who is now a law professor at the University of Utah, argues that the very absence of evidence is itself evidence. "My view is that there is no documented case of an innocent person that has been executed in this century," he says. If it had happened, surely by now capital punishment's many opponents would be able to produce a case. "I'm confident that the system is operating at close to the 100 per cent level of accuracy," he says.

But the absence of direct evidence may suggest nothing at all. When the defendant dies, his story dies with him, and the defense lawyers, many of them pro bono or state-appointed, move on to other cases. "Given that everyone's so strapped and there are so many cases," says Stephen B. Bright, the director of the Southern Center for Human Rights, an Atlanta-based aid group for poor defendants, "once they're dead, nobody's got time to spend on it." The original records and exhibits are destroyed or lost. Witnesses die or vanish, memories fade.

So we turn to indirect evidence. According to the Death Penalty Information Center, a group in Washington that opposes capital punishment, over the past 25 years 75 people have been released from death row and cleared of capital charges, out of about 6,000 who have been sentenced to die. Some won retrials and were acquitted; others were freed when new evidence turned up. Thus about 1 per cent of capital convictions turned out to be wrong.

The problem is that wrongful convictions tell us nothing about wrongful executions. Friends of the death penalty argue that the 75 releases show only that the system works. After all, the mistakes were corrected in time. Opponents argue that, human nature being what it is, there must be other mistakes that we didn't catch. In some cases, mistakes are found by mere chance. In 1996, two men on death row in Illinois were cleared after some journalism students looked into their case for a class assignment.

Not All Wrongful Convictions Are Rectified

Knowing the imperfection of all human institutions, a reasonable guess is that we catch many wrongful capital convictions, but not all of them. That, though, is just a guess—again, nothing solid. So we step back to look at the process itself. And here we find that it is quite careful, and that forensic technology—notably DNA testing—gets more precise all the time. On the other hand, most mistakes still flow from human error. Honest witnesses misremember, dishonest ones exchange false testimony for lenience, police or prosecutors make mistakes or become overzealous, appearances deceive.

In the legal process itself, moreover, any number of things can go wrong. For example, the law entitles the accused to a lawyer, but not a good one. Some jurisdictions simply contract out defense work to low-bidding attorneys, who spend as little time on each case as possible. Mississippi pays lawyers $1,000 plus expenses to represent capital defendants. Alabama pays defense lawyers $20 an hour, up to a limit of $2,000, to prepare capital cases, a job that can take hundreds of hours to do thoroughly. (Corporate lawyers receive as much as $500 an hour for their work in civil cases.) "Lawyers paid so little cannot afford to spend the time required to conduct interviews, investigations and negotiations," writes Bright. . . .

If you doubt that legal help matters, Bright points to a case in which two co-defendants, a man and a woman, were sentenced to death by unconstitutionally composed juries in Georgia. Her lawyers challenged the jury composition; his were unaware that they could do so. She got a retrial and a life sentence; he was executed in 1976.

As that case suggests, another sort of mistake may be fairly common, if less disturbing: A guilty person may be executed even though the jury would have voted for a milder sentence if it had had all the facts. We can be sure that this happens, because ex-jurors have come forward and said so. Or consider the extraordinary case of Jesse Dewayne Jacobs in Texas.

In 1987, Jacobs got death for his part in a plot to kidnap a woman named Etta Ann Urdiales and either terrorize her or kill her, depending on whom you believed. Urdiales ended up dead. Jacobs confessed to the murder but then recanted at trial, saying that he had been covering for his accomplice (and sister), Bobbie Hogan, who was the actual killer. The prosecutor wasn't buying it. He told the jury, "The simple fact of the matter is that Jesse Jacobs and Jesse Jacobs alone killed Etta Ann Urdiales." At Bobbie Hogan's trial a few months later, however, another prosecutor announced that the state had changed its mind, and that Hogan, not Jacobs, was the killer. Hogan, as it turned out, managed to convince the jury that the gun went off accidentally, and got 10 years for manslaughter. But meanwhile Jacobs appealed, arguing that if his jury had been told he was not the killer, it would have spared his life.

Texas, which accounts for almost half the country's executions, gave no ground. It argued that, under the state's murder law, a conspirator can get the death penalty even if he doesn't actually pull the trigger. The district attorney said, "This man was a sinister evil being who stalked this woman for two days, then broke into her house and beat the hell out of her. Even if he didn't do it himself, he knew a killing was going to take place." The Supreme Court declined Jacobs's appeal, and he died by lethal injection in 1995, protesting tearfully that he was innocent of the crime for which he would die. "There is not going to be an execution," he said. "This is premeditated murder.". . .

When you peel back the layers of procedure and law and anecdote and hunch, you find you can say no more than this: Usually, probably almost always, we kill the right person, but sometimes, probably quite rarely, we kill someone who does not deserve to die.

A Break for Jones?

In 1997, Leo Jones's defense lawyers got a couple of breaks—the sort of things that happen on TV. First, an investigator checked in with Schofield's friend Marion Manning, who mentioned that she had recently bumped into Shorty—Schofield's alibi witness—in jail. At last, a name surfaced: Roy Williams. In April, the defense lawyers talked to Shorty Williams, and he said that he was indeed with Schofield that night—and that he saw Schofield shoot Tom Szafranski. They had been driving in Manning's rental car. They both got out, and a little while later Williams saw Schofield fire at the police car from the bushes in the field across from Sixth and Davis.

Then, in the fall of 1997, something else happened. A recently retired Jacksonville police officer named Cleveland Smith, reading about Jones's claim that he had been beaten to confess, came to the defense lawyers with an ugly story. The officer who arrested Jones that night (and who was later pushed off the force) was known as an "enforcer," said Smith, "like a hit man on the police department."

Smith had seen the officer make up charges and torture a suspect with a pair of vise-grip pliers applied to the genitals. And, Smith recalled, this officer had told him of kicking down Jones's door on the fateful night intending "to kill somebody," and then badly beating a man. Finally, Smith reported that, at a roll call one day before the shooting, police officers were told that a man called "Mr. Jones" had fought with police. "We were told to do everything in our power to put Leo Jones in jail."

By this time—December 1997—no fewer than 10 prison inmates had reported hearing Glen Schofield boast of the killing. Six witnesses, four of them eyewitnesses, placed Schofield near the scene of the crime. Several said they had seen him with a rifle.

The defense was granted another evidentiary hearing, but in December a trial judge found against Jones. In March of 1998, for the fifth and last time, the Florida Supreme Court took up the case.

Death and Doubt

If we cannot say with any certainty which or how many people are wrongfully executed, perhaps we can at least find the right way to think about the problem. Begin with a question: Morally speaking, what sort of event is a mistaken execution?

At one extreme, maybe a wrongful execution is morally no better than a simple murder: the premeditated and wrongful killing of a person who does not deserve to die. But that can't be quite right. Murderers intend to take life wrongfully. That is precisely what we intend not to do, and take many precautions to avoid.

Perhaps, then, a wrongful execution is no more than an unfortunate but statistically inevitable accident, like a plane crash or a car wreck, and therefore a tragedy but not an injustice. After all, sometimes innocent civilians are killed in police chases, but we still chase criminals because, on balance, law enforcement is just and saves lives.

But that can't be right either. The innocent bystander killed in the police chase is not supposed to die, whereas the man wrongly executed was marched to the electric chair and destroyed on purpose. What was accidental in the latter case was not the killing but, so to speak, the innocence. Although many government policies are spoken of in terms of lives saved or lost, those are mathematical calculations that weigh statistical lives. For a liberal government, trading real people's lives for statistical ones is a treacherous game, even a wicked one. We kill statistical people every time we raise the speed limit, but that hardly entitles us to say, "In order to pass the bill reducing the speed limit and thus saving hundreds of lives, we will have to shoot three or four of the bill's opponents."

So wrongful execution lies somewhere between murder and mere accident. But where? Plainly, killing someone wrongfully is unjust, terribly so. Probably, however, most of us would say that if it happens only one time in a million—so we can execute a thousand people a year for a thousand years before making a mistake—then we should go ahead and punish the guilty. On the other hand, we would probably also say that if we killed one innocent man for every five guilty ones, that is too often.

But that sort of thinking is not helpful at all. First, it gives us no principled place to draw the line. How many wrongful deaths is too many—one in five? One in 20? One in 100? One in 1000? What possible moral grounds are there to support any number? The deeper problem, of course, is that in any case we have no idea what the number is, and we never will know.

Nowhere in American public policy is our ignorance so profound, so intractable. We cannot do the math, because there are no numbers. We cannot consult some morally similar case, because there is none. Somehow, we must decide without knowledge.

Perhaps the best we can hope for is some clarity about the sort of decision we face, and on that score it helps to get away from abstractions and statistics. Imagine a very crowded death row prison cell. Inside of it, by some miracle, are the 450 men and women who have been tried, condemned to death and executed since capital punishment was re-legalized in 1976. You are the governor, and you are standing outside the cell. You must execute them all or commute their sentences to life in prison. You know only two things.

First, most of the people in the cell, almost certainly the vast majority, are guilty of capital murder. They deserve to die.

Second, some of the people in the cell are innocent, meaning either that they did not commit the crime or do not deserve to die. You have no idea how many are innocent, or which ones they are, but your best guess is that the number is greater than zero but not huge.

To make the experiment a little more realistic, add some stipulations. As a nod to advocates of capital punishment, assume that by executing the people in this cell you will probably deter some future murders, although how many you have no idea. As a nod to the opponents of capital punishment, assume that the commuted sentence for all these people will be life without parole; none will ever walk the streets again (though some might kill in prison).

That is all you know or can know. Now you have a choice. If you pull the lever, someone innocent will die. If you fail to pull the lever, many murderers will live. What do you do?

It is not a trick question. There is no right answer, and any easy answer is wrong by definition. There is only the crowded cell, the uncertainty, and your moral intuition.

A Convicted Man Is Presumed Guilty

While the defense was busy in the Jones case, the state of Florida did not roll over and play dead. The prosecution investigated Jones's new witnesses and poked holes in their stories. The inmates to whom Schofield had allegedly confessed were hardly model citizens (one was serving 360 years for murder). The reported confessions were vague, bereft of telling detail. Boasting emptily of killing a cop is the sort of thing that a status-craving hood might well do in prison, especially if he knows that he can't actually be linked with the crime. In any case, the stuff was hearsay, of little or no use in court against Schofield's own denials.

As for the witnesses who reported seeing Schofield fleeing the scene with a rifle, some of them had records, too, and some were friends of Jones's, and Schofield's ex-girlfriend may have had a gripe with Schofield. And why had these people waited as long as 16 years to come forward? One of them had given an earlier affidavit without saying a thing about seeing Schofield.

Roy (Shorty) Williams was no perfect witness, either. In the affidavit he gave to Jones's defense counsel, he had described witnessing the crime as it actually occurred. But when the prosecutors took him to the crime scene (granted, this was 16 years after the shooting), he gave a different account, one that included fanciful details that didn't match the actual crime. He claimed Szafranski had parked his car in a place it couldn't have been, and that the deadly bullet entered through the car's side window rather than the front. In fact, Williams gave varying accounts, the only point of consistency being his insistence that he saw Schofield shoot from the field.

The alleged police brutality and forced confession were still just that, alleged. On the night when Jones was supposedly beaten, the doctor had found bruises and cuts but no serious injury. If these dreadful charges of police misconduct were true, why did Cleveland Smith wait so long to speak up? In any case, Smith's recollections were a long way from direct evidence that Jones's confession—produced hours after the alleged "enforcer" had left the scene—was coerced.

The state Supreme Court considered the issues from both substantive and legal points of view. Legally, a convicted man is presumed guilty. To protect the integrity of the original jury's decision, the law requires him to show, not merely that he might be innocent, but that his claims are new and haven't already been considered in court; that they would have been admissible as evidence at trial; and, not least, that if the jury had heard these claims, it would probably have acquitted.

Two of the court's seven justices said they would order a new trial for Jones. "Jones would probably be acquitted on retrial . . . in light of Officer Smith's testimony and the copious testimony implicating Schofield in the killing," said one. The other found that "the overwhelming volume" of the evidence implicating Schofield outweighed the inconsistencies between particular pieces.

The court's majority was not persuaded. It agreed with the state, and with the trial court, that the various items on Jones's roster of new evidence each failed one or more tests of substantive credibility or legal admissibility. For instance, the eyewitness testimony placing Schofield at the scene "probably would not have acquitted Jones" if it had been presented to the original jury. Even taking together all the testimony and Schofield's many alleged jailhouse confessions, "the only consistency over the years is the bare allegation of Schofield's involvement."

The court ruled: "No motion for rehearing will be heard."

Death and a Man

What do we know, really know, in the Jones case? We know that everyone involved with it knows what he, or she, believes. Angela B. Corey, the Florida assistant state attorney on the case, tells me that she needs no lectures on the importance of sparing innocent life. I ask about some of the framed pictures of children that clutter her Jacksonville office. Many are murder victims. "There was no one on our side of this that ever had one second's doubt that Leo Jones was guilty," she says, her eyes fierce. "Trust me, there is no one here who would have let Leo Jones die if we had thought there was any possibility he was innocent."

To visit Jones's defense lawyer, amid stacks of file boxes in a spartan office, is to enter another world. Martin J. McClain, of Florida's Capital Collateral Regional Counsel, the state agency that represents death row convicts on appeal, speaks wearily, with notes of resignation and despair. "I *know* that Leo Jones was innocent," he says, "and I know that either the system didn't work or I failed him."

The rest of us occupy yet a third world, a twilit place of doubt, where the only certainty is uncertainty. In the Jones case, the legal process worked as it was supposed to. Jones got a fair trial, he got competent lawyers, the prosecution cut square corners, the appeals were plentiful. Yet at the end of the day, fairness and knowledge are not the same thing. We do not know what happened at the corner of Sixth and Davis on the morning of May 23, 1981. We will never know.

> Very few people both defend capital punishment and take really seriously the problem of wrongful execution. John Stuart Mill was one of the few who did, and who understood knowledge's limits. The answer he proposed in 1868 may well have been the right one, or anyway as close to right as imperfect beings get. Here is what he said: "In order that the possibility of correction may be kept open wherever the chance of this sad contingency is more than infinitesimal, it is quite right that the judge should recommend to the crown a commutation of the sentence, not solely when the proof of guilt is open to the smallest suspicion, but whenever there remains anything unexplained and mysterious in the case, raising a

desire for more light, or making it likely that further information may at some future time be obtained. . . .

Clemency and Politics

Death row clemency, once quite common, now is a political death
sentence for governors. According to Richard C. Dieter of the Death
Penalty Information Center in Washington, in the 1990s clemency
has been granted in about one case a year.

We also know that in capital cases there is an inherent tradeoff
between meticulous thoroughness and reasonable speed, and that the
public's patience with long-delayed executions reached its limits a few
years ago and is now bouncing back, hard. Recent Supreme Court decisions have limited some lines of appeal, and the 1996 Anti-Terrorism
and Effective Death Penalty Act went the Supreme Court one better,
imposing many new restrictions on death row inmates' access to federal courts. In recent years, the average time between sentencing and
execution has been almost nine years; Dieter thinks new federal and
state laws may reduce the wait to three or four years. Moreover, one of
the first things the new Republican Congress did in 1995 was end federal funding to help pay for death row inmates' legal appeals. Thus in
Alabama today, according to Bryan A. Stevenson of the Equal Justice
Initiative, a legal-aid group in Montgomery, 18 death row convicts
have no lawyers at all—and, under the 1996 law, the clock is ticking
on their one-year deadline to file appeals. "Right now we have no
leads on counsel for any of these folks," Stevenson said. "Each week
becomes more desperate." Plainly, the public is not in the mood for
greater caution or more clemency.

Another possibility, of course, is abolition. That approach simply
says: There is one sort of mistake that a liberal government forswears
the right to make. This answer cuts the knot of wrongful execution,
but it means that justice will not be done for many killers. It means
living with Timothy McVeigh, a young man who, if he is spared, will
probably outlive most people reading this article.

Either course is imperfect, but both are more defensible than doing
as we do now: plunging deeper into the fog, hoping that mistakes don't
happen, and preferring not to think too hard about the whole problem.
True, we always make public choices in the face of uncertainty, even in
matters of life and death. But when we launch a military operation, we
acknowledge frankly that some good and innocent people will be
killed. And if we push on with more death sentences and fewer lines of
appeal, we must likewise say frankly: "Yes, in this country we sometimes execute innocent citizens, and in fact we are removing rather
than adding safeguards; but you have to break a few eggs to make an
omelet." Few Americans are willing to be quite so frank. They prefer to
assume that the convicted are guilty, so get on with it.

What to do? Again there is no right answer, and any easy answer is wrong by definition. But another thought experiment, a cell again. This time, however, the cell is not crowded; there is only one occupant, this time not a statistic but a person, a story. The man's name is Leo Alexander Jones—or, if you prefer, he is named something else, but the mystery is equivalent.

Do you pull the switch?

Epilogue

On March 24, 1998, Leo Alexander Jones said an Islamic prayer and died in the electric chair. He was the 15th person to be executed that year. Glen Schofield remains in prison in Florida.

One Man's Long Battle on Death Row

Tena Jamison Lee

Tena Jamison Lee is a legal affairs writer in Little Rock, Arkansas. In this article, she discusses the case of Joe Spaziano, who was convicted of killing Laura Lynn Harberts in Florida in 1973. Although Spaziano was sentenced to die for this crime, he has received more than one stay of execution because those who believe in his innocence have kept his case in the public spotlight. At the time that this article was originally published, Spaziano had already served twenty years in prison.

Maybe it was his unfortunate nickname, or maybe it was a community's bloodlust for revenge, but whatever it was, "Crazy" Joe Spaziano has spent the past 20 years in prison, possibly an innocent man.

Convicted of the 1973 murder of 18-year-old Laura Lynn Harberts, Spaziano has come within inches of being executed by a system that seemed to repeatedly and almost blatantly overlook one crucial point. Save for the testimony of a 16-year-old who held a grudge and "remembered" key facts under hypnosis, the state of Florida had no credible evidence against Spaziano.

"Regardless of what people think about the death penalty in the abstract, it does in fact send innocent people to death row and will, in fact, execute an innocent person," stressed Michael Mello, University of Vermont law professor and former public defender.

Believing "in the very marrow of my bones" that Spaziano is innocent, Mello says this case is a perfect example of a legal system gone awry. He's been involved in the case since the fall of 1983. Working with him to right this possible wrong is Stephen Hanlon, a partner at Holland & Knight, and co-chair of the IR&R Section's Committee on Civil Rights and Equal Opportunity.

Mello and Hanlon are quick to share credit, not only with the dogged determination of defense attorneys and judges, but to the involvement and down-right advocacy of *The Miami Herald*, which appears to have shamed the court system for now into preventing the execution.

"Joe Spaziano would not be alive today if not for *The Miami Her-*

Reprinted from "Anatomy of a Death Penalty Case: Did Florida Almost Execute an Innocent Man?" by Tena Jamison Lee, *Human Rights*, vol. 23, no. 3, Summer 1996. Reprinted by permission.

ald," said Hanlon. "This was not allowed to take place in the dead of the night as so many executions do."

The fact that this former death row inmate owes his life to a Florida newspaper is just one of many disturbing aspects of a case that spans 20 years.

On Aug. 21, 1973, the badly decomposed bodies of two women were spotted by a pool digger in a Seminole County trash dump. Some reports said the bodies were badly mutilated. One body was identified as Harberts, a hospital clerk who had a penchant for hitch-hiking. The other body has never been identified.

Most of the initial investigation centered around one suspect, Lynwood Tate, who had been arrested by police in his hometown of Athens, Ga., after he was accused of rape by an Orlando woman. Bank receipts showed that he opened a bank account in Orlando around the time of the Harberts disappearance. He also applied for a job at the hospital Harberts had worked at.

Tate was interrogated, underwent a polygraph test and was hypnotized. He failed a lie detector test and the investigator concluded in a report that everything, "indicated strongly that Lynwood Tate did commit the murder of Laura Lynn Harberts and the other unidentified female." Tate was never charged but remained a suspect until 1974.

Induced Testimony

In 1974, investigators began talking to Tony DiLisio, a 16-year-old drug user who admired Joe Spaziano's status as a chapter president of the Outlaws, an infamous motorcycle gang. They believed Spaziano may have been having a tumultuous affair with DiLisio's stepmother. She had once told a reporter that she was raped by Spaziano, but didn't press charges.

When first interrogated by police, DiLisio wasn't much help, saying he didn't know about the murders. Investigators apparently weren't convinced and decided to have him hypnotized by Joseph McCawley, a local fellow whose work has been questioned in the past.

After being hypnotized twice, DiLisio said he remembered Spaziano showing him two dead bodies. The induced testimony was just what prosecutors were waiting for. They proceeded with their case.

At the trial in January of 1976, DiLisio "remembered" that Spaziano had taken him to the dump to show him the two mutilated bodies and bragged of killing them. The jury was not told that these "recollections" were induced by hypnosis.

Most of DiLisio's testimony was inconsistent and went unchallenged by defense attorney Ed Kirkland. Initially, DiLisio said he was taking the drug LSD when he saw the bodies. At the trial, he said he didn't use any LSD until after he saw the bodies. He also gave testimony that conflicted with what he previously recounted about what he saw at the dump site.

Noting that their case hinged on his testimony, the prosecutor told the court, "if we can't get in the testimony of Tony DiLisio, we'd have absolutely no case whatsoever." They offered no physical evidence linking Spaziano to the murder.

After a lengthy deliberation, the jury returned with a guilty verdict. They recommended life in prison, a sentence that could indicate they didn't believe firmly in Spaziano's guilt: if they thought he committed this brutal crime, they probably would have sentenced him to death.

Mello has a juror affidavit stating that the jury recommended life imprisonment rather than death because they weren't so certain that Spaziano was guilty at all. The jury's only choices at the guilt/innocence stage were acquittal or conviction of first degree murder.

At trial, Spaziano's Outlaw biker colleagues sported full biker regalia, tattoos and all. Jurors weren't so sure they wanted to let Spaziano back on the streets. They opted to put him in prison for life.

Judge Robert McGregor overrode their recommendation and sentenced Spaziano to the death penalty.

Problems with the Case

Mello was assigned to Spaziano's case in the fall of 1983 while at the Office of the Capital Collateral Representative.

"I thought that the trial was a joke—as screwed up as any I'd read about," says Mello who is one of a handful of specialists in post-conviction homicide law and has represented some 70 condemned men, including confessed serial murderer Ted Bundy.

"When I first get involved in a case, guilt and innocence are irrelevant to me." After meeting his client a year later, Mello was convinced of his innocence. "He had this straightforward way about him."

Three key issues jumped out at Mello when reviewing the case, and still trouble him today:

• It violated the federal constitution to permit judges to override a jury recommendation of life imprisonment.

Mello raised the issue in a certiorari petition to the U.S. Supreme Court, which granted cert in the spring of 1984. Since the jury usually represents a cross section of the community, they are perhaps more sympathetic, he argued. He pointed to a study that found when judges are elected, they tend to be more death penalty prone, especially in high profile cases.

Furthermore, he maintained, the death decision is a moral judgment, not a legal judgment.

He lost his argument.

The U.S. Supreme Court upheld the conviction 6–3 with justices Brennan, Marshall and Stevens dissenting. The dissenting judges reasoned that it is cruel and unusual punishment for a judge to overrule a jury and impose a death sentence on his own.

Florida is one of four states including Indiana, Alabama and

Delaware, that allows a judge to override a jury's sentence. Since the responsibility of sentencing was divided between the judge and the jury, neither had responsibility for Spaziano's life.

It didn't help that Spaziano was feared and loathed by the community, and the *Orlando Sentinel* clamored for his death.

A judge can override a jury when "no reasonable juror could have ever come to that conclusion." Based on the available evidence, Hanlon is surprised the judge came to the death penalty conclusion.

"We have a horrendous problem here in Florida," agrees Hanlon. "Jury overrides are routinely upheld in Florida . . . and it has worked the opposite of what the law intended."

• The key witness in the Spaziano trial revealed information only under hypnosis.

In the 1985 case, *Bundy v. State of Florida*, the Florida Supreme Court ruled that hypnosis–induced evidence is unreliable and inadmissible. The Florida Supreme Court refused to apply its 1985 decision to Spaziano's case.

• The jury was never told that DiLisio's memory was "enhanced" by hypnosis.

Undisclosed Evidence

In October 1984, the governor signed Spaziano's first execution order. Mello won a stay of execution, although the Florida Supreme Court later rejected his argument. This argument centered around the prosecution's failure to disclose evidence to Spaziano's trial attorney that someone else may have been implicated in the murder.

Prosecutors introduced into evidence that Harberts' roommate heard her speaking to a "Joe" on the phone the night she disappeared.

What police and prosecutors knew, but didn't disclose, was that Harberts was talking to a coworker and known sex offender, Joe Suarez, not Joe Spaziano. Mello also learned after Spaziano's first trial that Suarez denied to the police that he had been with Harberts on August 5, 1973, just weeks before her body was found.

More importantly, in an undisclosed documented interview, police were able to conclude that Suarez was with Harbert on the night of her disappearance.

Mello failed to persuade the state trial judge, the justices of the Florida Supreme Court, a federal district judge, three judges on the Eleventh Circuit Court of Appeals, and the Justices of the U.S. Supreme Court to look at any of this new evidence.

In 1994, he filed another certiorari petition with the U.S. Supreme Court, to no avail.

"It is a court rule that if the defense attorney did not make proper objections during the trial, then the error cannot be raised on appeal. Also, federal courts must defer to state procedural rules. Because of this, no court has ever ruled on the merits of the evidence demonstrating Mr. Spaziano's innocence," wrote Mello in the 1995 Fall *Vermont Law Review.*

On May 24, 1995, Florida Gov. Chiles signed another death warrant for Spaziano. His execution date was set for 7 a.m., June 27, 1995.

The Media Gets Involved

Feeling defeated by the courts, Mello decided to do something he swore he would never do. He took his case to the media.

He had admired the Pulitzer Prize–winning book, *Invitation to a Lynching,* by *Miami Herald* senior editor Gene Miller, which traces the story of Freddie Pitts and Wilbert Lee, who were innocent of their crimes.

Mello pleaded with Miller, who finally agreed to review the case. Miller combed through trial transcripts, police reports, transcripts of the hypnosis sessions of the state's star witness, and audio tapes of those hypnosis sessions. He then passed the information over to Warren Holmes, who had been his chief investigator in the Pitts and Lee case.

Both Miller and Holmes came to believe that Spaziano was innocent.

With only a month left before the execution date, the newspaper assigned a bevy of reporters to attack the story from all angles. They began with tracking down Tony DiLisio.

In 1985, Mello sent his own investigator to a small California town where DiLisio lived, but DiLisio wouldn't talk. Ten years later, in March of 1995, an investigator from the Capital Collateral Representative office (where Mello worked) found DiLisio in Pensacola, Florida. He still wouldn't talk.

Mello finally gave the Pensacola address to *Miami Herald* reporter Lori Rozsa, whose first encounter with DiLisio ended with a curt slamming of his door in her face. She tried two more times, but couldn't get him to talk.

Finally, on her fourth visit to his door, DiLisio opened up, inviting Rozsa into is kitchen and confessing to her that the police had pressured him to finger Spaziano 20 years earlier.

He told of being offered his freedom from a juvenile facility in exchange for testifying against Spaziano. He told of his father's hatred toward Spaziano for having an affair with DiLisio's stepmother. He told of his willingness to do anything to please his abusive father. He told of finding God and wanting to clear his conscience. It was just the story the *Herald* (and Spaziano) needed.

Rozsa wrote of the recantation and subsequent stories championing Spaziano's innocence. Other media began to pick up the story and champion Spaziano's cause of being falsely accused. *The Orlando Sentinel,* however, fought tooth and nail for Spaziano's execution.

Pressured by media reports, Governor Chiles stayed the June 27 execution and ordered a state investigation by the Florida Department of Law Enforcement into DiLisio's recantation. The report, which was sealed, nevertheless challenged whether DiLisio's recantation was credible.

Chiles signed a new death warrant on August 24, 1995, Spaziano's fifth.

On September 8, Mello approached the Florida Supreme Court requesting a stay of execution and an evidentiary hearing. The stay was denied, but the hearing was granted.

The court ordered Mello, an appellate lawyer with very little trial experience, no associates and no investigator, to handle an evidentiary hearing one week later. The court also ordered the Capital Collateral Representative office to assist.

Mello argued that a week was not enough time.

On September 12, 1995, the court threw Mello off the case and granted Spaziano another stay. An evidentiary hearing to explore DiLisio's recanted testimony was scheduled for the second week of January 1996.

Enter Hanlon and Holland & Knight, Florida's largest law firm with 475 lawyers strong. Led by Gregg Thomas, a partner of the firm's Tampa office, along with Jim Russ, a prominent Orlando criminal defense lawyer, the team quickly assembled to explore the single issue of DiLisio's recantation. The Thanksgiving and Christmas holidays flashed by them unnoticed.

"We worked day and night on this case," admitted Hanlon. "An enormous effort is involved in a death penalty case. All circumstances surrounding his testimony needed to be investigated."

Two expert witnesses on repressed memory were called, as well as DiLisio himself who stood by his recantation. The firm donated about $400,000 in lawyer time as well as $400,000 in costs to handle the hearing. The time and money apparently paid off.

Gearing Up for Another Trial

One day before the 20th anniversary of the murder conviction that sent Spaziano to death row, Florida circuit court judge O.H. Eaton, Jr., ordered a new murder trial for Spaziano.

"In the United States of America every person, no matter how unsavory, is entitled to due process of law and a fair trial. The defendant received neither," Eaton wrote in an eight-page ruling. "The validity of the verdict in this case rests upon the testimony of an admitted perjurer who had every reason to fabricate a story which he hoped would be believed."

The state has decided to appeal the decision to the Florida Supreme Court and recently filed an initial brief in the case.

As both sides gear up for another round, Spaziano waits in prison, although now off of death row. He is serving time for a rape conviction that also hinges on the testimony of Tony DiLisio.

If his persistent attorneys and supporters have their way, Spaziano may some day become a free man.

CHAPTER 5

IMPLEMENTING THE DEATH PENALTY: PERSONAL NARRATIVES

SENDING A MAN TO DIE

Alex Kozinski

Alex Kozinski serves as a judge on the United States Court of Appeals for the Ninth Circuit. In the following essay, Kozinski reflects on the first occasion in which he had to decide whether to approve a stay of execution for a condemned murderer. Kozinski describes the reasoning that led him to oppose the stay, including his belief that the execution would provide a measure of justice for the murder victim. Yet despite his strong approval of the death penalty, Kozinski reveals, his conflicting feelings about its efficacy and morality increasingly bothered him as the execution drew nigh. Although he continues to support the death penalty, the author makes it clear that judges bear a heavy burden in their ability to decide between life and death.

I woke with a start and sat upright in the darkness.

He must be dead by now.

The thought filled my head and gave me a weird sense of relief. But no, it couldn't be. The execution was set for Sunday morning at seven—long after daybreak. The display on the digital clock showed 1:23. I fell back on my pillow and tried to chase Thomas Baal from my mind.

I had first heard his name just three days earlier. My friend and mentor Supreme Court Justice Anthony M. Kennedy had mentioned during a telephone conversation that an execution was scheduled that night somewhere in my jurisdiction. As a judge on the United States Court of Appeals for the Ninth Circuit, I hear cases from nine states and two territories spread over the Western United States and Oceania.

"Must not be mine," I told him, "or I'd have heard about it by now." And left for lunch. When I returned, the fax was chattering away.

"The clerk's office called," my secretary said. "Guess who's been drawn for that execution?"

"How can it be? A man is scheduled to die tonight and this is the first I hear of it?"

"He doesn't want a stay," my law clerk interjected. "I've been reading the documents and it looks like he's ready to swallow the bitter pill. It's his mom and dad who are trying to stop the execution. They

Excerpted from "Tinkering with Death," by Alex Kozinski, *The New Yorker*, vol. 72, no. 46, February 10, 1997. Reprinted by permission of the author.

say he's not competent to waive his right to appeal. The district court is holding a hearing even as we speak."

"Oh, good," I muttered. "Maybe the district judge will enter a stay."

"Fat chance," my secretary and my law clerk said in unison. "Better read those papers."

Brutal Facts

As I drifted back to sleep, I thought that Thomas Baal was not such a bad fellow compared with some of his neighbors on death row. On February 26, 1988, Baal had robbed thirty-four-year-old Frances Maves at knifepoint. Maves gave him twenty dollars, but Baal demanded more. She struggled. "You shouldn't have done that," Baal told her. "Now you pay. I sentence you to death." He stabbed Maves eight times.

I had seen my first death cases shortly after law school, when I clerked at the United States Supreme Court for former Chief Justice Warren E. Burger. That was almost two decades ago now, but I've never quite gotten over the experience. Whatever qualms I had about the efficacy or the morality of the death penalty were drowned out by the pitiful cries of the victims screaming from between the lines of dry legal prose:

> On the afternoon of May 14, 1973, defendant and three oth- ers . . . drove to the residence of Jerry Alday. . . . The defen- dant and one of his companions entered the mobile home for the purpose of burglary. Shortly thereafter two members of the Alday family, Jerry and his father, Ned Alday, arrived in a jeep, were escorted at gunpoint into the trailer, and were shot to death at close range with handguns. . . .

> Shortly thereafter a tractor driven by Jerry's brother, Jimmy Alday, arrived at the trailer. After being forced to empty his pockets, he was placed on the living room sofa and killed with a handgun fired at close range.

> While one of the four was moving the tractor out of the dri- veway, Jerry's wife, Mary, arrived at her home by car. . . . Two other members of the Alday family, Aubrey and Chester, Jerry's uncle and brother, arrived in a pickup truck. Mary was forced into the bathroom while Aubrey and Chester were taken at gunpoint into the bedrooms and shot in a manner similar to the first two victims. . . .

> Mary Alday was then raped by two or more of the men. . . . She was then taken, bound and blindfolded, in her car about six miles to a wooded area where she was raped by two of the

men, was beaten when she refused to commit oral sodomy, and her breasts mutilated. She was then killed with two shots. Her watch was then removed from her nude body.

Sometimes the victims had tiny voices, barely audible as they endured fates so horrible that they defy human comprehension:

Over the . . . latter portion of Kelly Ann's short, torturous life the defendant [her father] did these things to her on one or many occasions:

1. Beat her in the head until it was swollen.

2. Burned her hands.

3. Poked his fingers in her eyes.

4. Beat her in the abdomen until "it was swollen like she was pregnant."

6. Held her under water in both the bath tub and toilet.

7. Kicked her against a table which cut her head then . . . sewed up her wound with needle and thread.

9. On one occasion beat her continuously for 45 minutes.

13. Choked her on the night she died and when she stopped breathing . . . placed her body in a plastic garbage bag and buried her in an unmarked and unknown grave.

Brutal facts have immense power; they etched deep marks in my psyche. Those who commit such atrocities, I concluded, forfeit their own right to live. We tarnish the memory of the dead and heap needless misery on their surviving families by letting the perpetrators live.

Still, it's one thing to feel and another to do. It's one thing to give advice to a judge and quite another to *be* the judge signing the order that will lead to the death of another human being—even a very bad one. Baal was my first.

In the Court's Hands

Another start. The clock showed 3 A.M. Would this night never end? I knew I had done the right thing; I had no doubts. Still, I wished it were over.

The district court had made its decision around 6 P.M. Thursday. Yes, Baal was competent; he could—and did—waive his right to all appeals, state and federal. This finding was based on the affidavits of the psychiatrists who had examined Baal, and on Baal's courtroom responses:

The Court: Do you want us to stop [the execution], sir, to give you an opportunity to appeal . . .?

The Defendant: No, I feel that I've gone through a lot of problems in there and I'm just—I feel that the death penalty is needed. And I don't feel that I have to stick around ten years and try to fight this thing out because it's just not in me.

The Court: You know that your act here in the Courtroom of saying, "Don't stop the execution," will result in your death. You're aware of that, are you not?

The Defendant: Yes. . . .

The Court: Now, you know that the choice that you're making here is either life or death. Do you understand that?

The Defendant: I understand. I choose death. . . .

The Court: Is there anything else?

The Defendant: Just bring me a hooker.

The Court: Obviously the court can't grant requests such as that. Any other requests?

The Defendant: Just my last meal and let's get the ball rolling.

In desperation, Baal's parents had submitted an affidavit from a psychiatrist who, without examining Baal, could say only that he *might* not be competent. The district judge didn't buy it. Stay denied.

The case officially landed in my lap just as I was leaving the office for dinner at a friend's house. I arranged with the two other judges who had been selected to hear the case for a telephone conference with the lawyers later that evening. Nothing stops the conversation at a dinner party quite like the half-whispered explanation "I have to take this call. It's a stay in a death case. Don't hold dessert."

Last-minute stay petitions in death cases are not unusual; they're a reflex. Except in rare cases where the prisoner decides to give up his appeal rights, death cases are meticulously litigated, first in state court and then in federal court—often bouncing between the two systems several times—literally until the prisoner's dying breath. Once the execution date is set, the process takes on a frantic pace. The death warrant is usually valid only for a limited time—in some states only for a single day—and the two sides battle furiously over that piece of legal territory.

If the condemned man . . . can delay the execution long enough for the death warrant to expire, he will have bought himself a substantial reprieve—at least a few weeks, sometimes months or years. But, if the state can carry out the execution, the game ends in sudden death and the prisoner's arguments die with him.

The first time I had seen this battle was in 1977, when a platoon of American Civil Liberties Union lawyers descended on the United States Supreme Court in a vain effort to save Gary Gilmore's life. Gilmore's case was pivotal to death-penalty opponents, because he would be the first to be executed since the Supreme Court had emptied the nation's death rows in 1972 by declaring all existing death-penalty statutes unconstitutional. A number of states had quickly retooled their death statutes, but opponents hoped to use procedural delays to stave off all executions for many years. Gilmore upset this calculation by waiving his appeals after he was found guilty.

Gilmore was scheduled to face the firing squad on the morning of January 17, 1977. Efforts to obtain a stay from the lower federal courts during the night had proved unsuccessful, and the lawyers brought a stack of papers to the Supreme Court Clerk's office. The Court was due to hear cases at ten, which was also when the execution was scheduled. In the hour before the Justices took the bench, Michael Rodak, the Clerk of the Supreme Court, carried the petition to them in their chambers—first to one, then to another. The Justices entered the courtroom at the stroke of ten, and Rodak hurried back to his office. A few minutes after ten, he placed a call to the state prison in Draper, Utah, where Gilmore was being held. He first identified himself with a password: "This is Mickey from Wheeling, West Virginia." He continued, "I've presented the stay petition to the Justices, and it was denied. You may proceed with the execution."

Rodak then fell silent for a few seconds as he listened to the response from the other end of the line.

"Oh. . . . You mean he's already dead?"

Resisting Manipulation of the Law

So as not to wake my wife with my tossing, I went to the kitchen and made myself a cup of tea. As I sipped the hot liquid, I thumbed through the small mountain of papers that had accumulated over the past seventy-two hours.

With the stakes in death cases so high, it's hard to escape the feeling of being manipulated, the suspicion that everything the lawyers say or do is designed to entice or intimidate you into giving them what they want. Professional distance—the detachment that is the lawyers' stock-in-trade in ordinary cases—is absent in death cases. It's the battle of the zealots.

And it's not just the lawyers. Death cases—particularly as the execution draws near—distort the deliberative process and turn judges into advocates. There are those of my colleagues who have never voted to uphold a death sentence and doubtless never will. The view that judges are morally justified in undermining the death penalty, even though it has been approved by the Supreme Court, was legitimatized by the former Supreme Court Justices William J. Brennan, Jr., and Thurgood Marshall, who voted to vacate as cruel and unusual every single death sentence that came before the Court. Just before retiring, in 1994, Justice Harry A. Blackmun adopted a similar view, by pronouncing, "From this day forward, I shall no longer tinker with the machinery of death."

Refusing to enforce a valid law is a violation of the judges' oath—something that most judges consider a shameful breach of duty. But death is different, or so the thinking goes, and to slow down the pace of executions by finding fault with every death sentence is considered by some to be highly honorable. In the words of Justice Brennan, this practice "embod[ies] a community striving for human dignity for all, although perhaps not yet arrived."

Judges like me, who support the death penalty, are swept right along. Observing manipulation by the lawyers and complicity from liberal colleagues, conservative judges often see it as their duty to prevent death-row inmates from diminishing the severity of their sentence by endlessly postponing the day of reckoning. . . .

Delaying Executions Is Inhumane

Another hour passed, but sleep eluded me. Events of the last three days kept knocking around in my head.

Over my friend's kitchen telephone, the lawyers spoke with great urgency and took predictable positions. Afterward, my colleagues and I conferred. One of them—who has never seen a death sentence he liked—quickly voted to issue a stay. Almost instinctively, I took the opposite view. After some discussion, the third judge voted for a stay, and the execution was halted.

We spent all day Friday and most of that night preparing the stay order and my dissent. My colleagues argued that Baal's parents made a strong showing that he was not competent to surrender his life: he had a long history of "behavioral and mental problems," had attempted suicide on several occasions, and had been found to suffer from a variety of psychiatric disorders. Twice in the past, he had waived his legal remedies but had later changed his mind.

My dissent emphasized the diagnosis of the psychiatrists who had examined him; the state court's finding—just a week earlier—that he was competent; and Baal's lucid and appropriate answers to questions posed from the bench. I ended by arguing that Baal's decision to forgo the protracted trauma of numerous death-row appeals was rational, and that my colleagues were denying his humanity by refusing to accept his decision:

It has been said that capital punishment is cruel and unusual because it is degrading to human dignity. . . . But the dignity of human life comes not from mere existence, but from that ability which separates us from the beasts—the ability to choose; freedom of will. *See* Immanuel Kant, "Critique of Pure Reason." When we say that a man—even a man who has committed a horrible crime—is not free to choose, we take away his dignity just as surely as we do when we kill him. Thomas Baal has made a decision to accept society's punishment and be done with it. By refusing to respect his decision we denigrate his status as a human being.

The idea that a long sojourn on death row is itself an excruciating punishment—and violates basic human rights—has gained some notable adherents. In 1989, the European Court of Human Rights refused to order the extradition of a man wanted for murder in the United States on the ground that the delay in carrying out death sentences in this country amounts to inhuman and degrading punishment. Four years later, the British Privy Council vacated a Jamaican death sentence because its imposition had been delayed for fourteen years. The Supreme Court of Zimbabwe reached a similar conclusion with respect to much shorter delays—delays that were, however, coupled with unusually harsh conditions of confinement.

This view has some important followers in the United States as well, notably Supreme Court Justice John Paul Stevens. Justice Stevens argues that such delayed executions violate the Constitution, because they serve no purpose. Living for twenty years under the terror of a death sentence is punishment enough, he argues; moreover, a death sentence so long delayed can have no deterrent value and is therefore capricious. No other Justice has yet embraced this view, but Justice Stephen G. Breyer has shown some sympathy.

There is a lot to be said, of course, for the proposition that the death penalty ought to be carried out swiftly. But swift justice is hard to come by, because the Supreme Court has constructed a highly complex—and mutually contradictory—series of conditions that must be satisfied before a death sentence may be carried out. On the one hand, there must be individual justice: there can be no mandatory death sentence, no matter how heinous the crime. On the other hand, there must be consistent justice: discretion to impose the death penalty must be tightly circumscribed. But individual justice is inherently inconsistent—different juries reach different results in similar cases. And there are scores of other issues that arise in every criminal case but take on special significance when death is involved. Death, as liberal judges keep telling us, is different.

Not surprisingly, a good lawyer (with cover from sympathetic judges) can postpone an execution for many years. When Duncan Peder McKenzie reached the end of the road on May 10, 1995, he had been a fixture of Montana's death row for two decades. A total of forty-one state and federal judges had examined the case (many of them several times) and had issued two dozen published opinions analyzing various claims. In the end, McKenzie argued that he had suffered enough because of this delay and he should be forgiven his death sentence. We rejected this argument, and the Supreme Court refused to stay the execution, with Justice Stevens dissenting.

A Sense of Unease

Dawn broke as I drifted off into fitful sleep, but a part of me kept reaching out to the man I knew was living the last hour of his life. Awareness of death is intrinsic to the human condition, but what is it like to know precisely—to the minute—when your life is going to end? Does time stand still? Does it race? How can you swallow, much less digest, that last meal? Or even think of hookers?

Though I've now had a hand in a dozen or more executions, I have never witnessed one. The closest I came was a conversation with Bill Allen, a lawyer from my former law firm. I ran into him at a reception and his face was gray, his eyes—usually sharp and clear—seemed out of focus.

"Not well," Bill answered when I asked how he was doing. "I lost a client. His name was Linwood Briley. I saw him die in the electric chair a couple of days ago."

"Was it rough?"

"What do you think? It was awful."

"What was it like when they turned on the juice?"

"Oh, by the time they got done strapping him down, putting the goop on his head and the mask on his face, the thing sitting in that chair hardly looked human. But the really strange part was before: looking at him, talking to him, even joking with him, fully aware he'd be dead in half an hour."

"Why did you go?"

"I thought he should have a friend there with him in his final minutes."

The look on Bill's face stayed with me a long time. It was enough to persuade me that I'd never want to witness an execution. Yet I sometimes wonder whether those of us who make life-and-death decisions on a regular basis should not be required to watch as the machinery of death grinds up a human being. I ponder what it says about me that I can, with cool precision, cast votes and write opinions that seal another human being's fate but lack the courage to witness the consequences of my actions.

After filing my dissent, at 2:59 A.M. Saturday, I put Baal out of my mind, figuring that it would be quite some time before I'd have to think about him again. Much to my surprise, however, the Supreme Court issued an order that evening, lifting our stay. The execution was on. The Court had more or less adopted my reasoning—even cited me by name. I felt triumphant.

But, as Saturday turned to night, it began to sink in that Baal really *was* going to die, and that I would have played a part in ending his life. The thought took hold of my mind and would not let go. It filled me with a nagging sense of unease, something like motion sickness.

I finally plunged into a deep sleep from which I awoke long after the execution was over. I was grateful not to have been awake to imagine in real time how Baal was strapped onto a gurney, how his vein was opened, how the deadly fluids were pumped into his body.

Lethal injection, which has overtaken the electric chair as the execution method of choice, is favored because it is sure, painless, and nonviolent. But I find it creepy that we pervert the instruments of healing—the needle, the pump, the catheter, F.D.A.-approved drugs—by putting them to such an antithetical use. It also bothers me that we mask the most violent act that society can inflict on one of its members with such an antiseptic veneer. Isn't death by firing squad, with mutilation and bloodshed, more honest?

Alternative Methods?

Some three hundred and sixty people have been executed since Gary Gilmore. The most we have dispatched in any one year was fifty-six, in 1995. As of 1997, there are thirty-one hundred or so awaiting their date with the executioner, and the number is growing. Impatient with the delays, Congress passed the Effective Death Penalty Act in 1996, which will probably hasten the pace of executions. Even then, it's doubtful we have the resources or the will even to keep up with the three hundred or so convicted murderers we add to our death rows every year.

With the pace of executions quickening and the total number of executions rising, I fear it's only a matter of time before we learn that we've executed the wrong man. There have already been cases where prisoners on death row were freed after evidence turned up proving them innocent. I dread the day we are confronted with a case in which the conclusive proof of innocence turns up too late.

And I sometimes wonder whether the death penalty is not an expensive and distracting sideshow to our battle against violent crime. Has our national fascination with capital punishment diverted talent and resources from mundane methods of preventing violent crime? Take William Bonin, the notorious Freeway Killer, who raped, tortured, and murdered fourteen teen-age boys, then dumped their bodies along Southern California's freeways. If anyone deserved execution, surely it was Bonin. And on February 23, 1996, after fourteen years on death row, he went to his death, even then mocking the families of his victims. Asked if he had any regrets, the confessed killer admitted that, indeed, he did: "Well, probably I went in the [military] service too soon, because I was peaking in my bowling career. I was carrying, like, a 186 to a 190 average. . . . I've always loved bowling."

Yet, looking at the record in his case, one can't help noting that Bonin had given us ample warning of his proclivities. While serving in Vietnam, he had sexually assaulted at gunpoint two soldiers under his command. After returning to civilian life, he had been convicted of molesting four boys between the ages of twelve and eighteen. He had served three years for those crimes and, upon his release, molested another boy. Again, he had served only three years and had then been set free to commence his killing spree.

Bonin is not unique. My concurring opinion in his case lists a number of other killers who gave us fair warning that they were dangerous but were nevertheless set free to prey on an unsuspecting and vulnerable population. Surely putting to death ten convicted killers isn't nearly as useful as stopping a single Bonin before he tastes blood.

Listening to the Victims

It's late Saturday night. Another execution is scheduled for next week, and the machinery of death is humming through my fax. And, despite the qualms, despite the queasiness I still feel every time an execution is carried out in my jurisdiction, I tinker away. I do it because I have taken an oath. But there's more. I do it because I believe that society is entitled to take the life of those who have shown utter contempt for the lives of others. And because I hear the tortured voices of the victims crying out to me for vindication.

THE DEATH OF ROBERT ALTON HARRIS

Michael Kroll

Robert Alton Harris received the death penalty for murdering two teenagers in 1978. On April 21, 1992, he became the first person to be executed by lethal gas in California in twenty-five years. Michael Kroll, a contributing editor with the Pacific News Service, first met Harris in 1984 while working on an article about death row. In the following selection, Kroll describes how he served as a witness at his friend's execution. According to the author, Harris's friends and family members were treated differently than the witnesses from the victims' families. For instance, he writes, members of the victims' families were provided counseling while Harris's brother endured a humiliating strip search. Kroll also gives an emotional account of his reaction to watching the execution.

"Ladies and gentlemen. Please stay in your places until your escort comes for you. Follow your escort, as instructed. Thank you."

The words were spoken in the manner of the operator of the Jungle Cruise at Disneyland: well-rehearsed and "professional." They were spoken by San Quentin's public information officer, Vernell Crittendon, as we waited to be ushered out of the gas chamber where my friend Robert Harris was slumped over, dead, in Chair B.

When not conveying us to and from the gas chamber, our "escorts" guarded us in a small, tidy office with barred windows facing the east gate, where a circus of media lights lit up the night sky, letting us see silhouettes in the darkness. There were two desks, the exact number of straight-backed chairs needed to accommodate us, some nineteen-cent bags of potato chips, a couple of apples and bananas, and bad coffee.

We—a psychologist and lawyer who knew Robert Harris professionally, his brother Randy, whom he had designated to witness the gassing, and I, a close friend for nearly a decade—had entered at the west gate at 10 P.M. as instructed to present our credentials (a written

Reprinted from "The Unquiet Death of Robert Harris," by Michael Kroll, *The Nation*, July 6, 1992. Reprinted with permission of *The Nation*.

invitation from Warden Daniel Vasquez himself) and submit to a thorough pat-down search and a metal detector. Our escorts took us in a prison van to the front of the old fortress and escorted us up a few steps into the office of one G. Mosqueda, program administrator. Then we began what we thought at the time would be a short vigil. It turned out to be eight hours.

A Humiliating Process

We'd been there only a few minutes when another staff person arrived wearing a civilian suit and a name tag that identified him as Martinez. He walked up to Randy, pointed his finger and said, "Randall Harris. Come with me!" Randy smiled, got up and followed him out. (Randy told me later that he thought they were taking him for counseling. It was a fair assumption; counselors had been provided by the prison to advise members of the victims' families who had come to witness the execution. This was to insure, Warden Vasquez told them, that "there is only one casualty in that room.")

"Where have you taken Randy?" the lawyer asked as soon as he was gone. "I don't know," replied Mendez. "You'll have to ask Martinez." Mendez was our escort, you see. An escort only escorts. When they brought him back, he told his own horror story. He had been ordered to submit to a full body-cavity search. "We have learned from a reliable source that you are planning something," Martinez had said. Randy protested that he was there for his brother, a solemn responsibility he would rather not have. He asked who the "reliable source" was. "None of your business," he was told. He was ordered to take his clothes off, bend over, lift his testicles, pull back his foreskin. He had to open his mouth for inspection. "If you try anything," Martinez had threatened, "you'll be sorry, and so will your brother."

His brother was waiting just a few feet from the gas chamber.

After Randy rejoined us, shaken and humiliated, our escort gave us our marching orders. "When the phone rings and I get the order to go, stand and follow me quickly." The phone, which had the kind of clanging ring that scares you to death even when you are not already scared to death, rang many times that night and each time our hearts stopped. But *the* call did not come at midnight. It did not come for a long time. With no television to inform us, we waited, hour after hour, wondering what was happening, drinking bad coffee and asking to be escorted to the bathroom.

Later, we learned that in those hours the U.S. Court of Appeals for the Ninth Circuit had granted three stays of execution. One concerned newly discovered evidence that Robert's brother Danny, who had participated in the crime but served fewer than four years in exchange for his testimony against Robert, had actually fired the first shot. The two other stays—including one signed by ten judges—were based on the pending suit challenging the constitutionality of cyanide gas as a method of execution. Each of the three stays was dissolved by the Supreme Court.

Finally, a little after 3 o'clock, the call came and Mendez said, "Now."

The Gas Chamber

We followed him into the freezing, brilliant night, but Mendez stopped us just short of the entrance to the gas chamber. Shivering, we watched the other witnesses being led out of the cold—the media into one building opposite the gas chamber and the victims' family members into the East Block visiting room just beyond it. After a while, responding to words over his walkie-talkie I could not hear, Mendez led us into the main visiting room to our immediate right. I had been in this room many times, but never at night, and never, as now, was it deserted of staff and inmates.

(While we waited, unaware of the cause for the delay, prison officials were arguing fiercely about where to set up the video camera that Judge Patel had ordered to assist her in determining whether death by lethal gas is cruel and unusual punishment—an order that had been vigorously opposed by the attorney general. Just outside the entrance to the gas chamber, not ten feet from where I was pacing nervously and watching the clock, the man assigned by the defense team to operate the camera was met by San Quentin's public information officer. "How much time will it take you to set up?" Crittendon demanded. "Five minutes, or so," he was told. "We don't have five minutes," he yelled.)

And then the wait was over. Mendez spoke into his walkie-talkie. "Okay," he said, and then turned his attention to us. "Let's go."

We, the family and friends of the condemned, were led to risers along a wall behind and to the left of the chamber. Three burly guards brought Robert in and strapped him quickly to Chair B. His back was to us. He could see us only by craning his neck and peering over his left shoulder. From behind him, I looked over his right shoulder into the unblinking red eye of the video camera trained on his face. He peered around the room, making eye contact, smiling and nodding at people he knew. I held my breath. A guard's digital watch started beeping. She smiled sheepishly and covered it with her sleeve.

Minutes passed. Some people whispered. Some smiled. And then the phone rang. The phone to the gas chamber rings for only one reason: A stay of execution has been granted. But nothing happened. Nobody moved—nobody except Robert, that is, who twisted and turned trying to figure out what was happening. He peered down between his legs to see if he could see the vat of acid beneath him. He sniffed the air and mouthed the words, "Pull it." More minutes passed. He peered over his left shoulder where I was just out of his line of vision. "Where's Mike?" he mouthed.

I jumped down to the lower riser and walked over to the window. A female guard ordered me back to my place, but not before Robert saw me, smiled and settled down.

An Unusual Event

Ten minutes after the phone rang, the gas chamber door was opened and the three guards unfastened Robert and took him from the chamber. Nothing like that had ever happened in the history of the gas chamber. (I later learned that during that eternity, California's Attorney General, Dan Lungren, had been on the phone to the clerk of the U.S. Supreme Court informing him that Robert was in the chamber. Lungren begged the Justices to overturn the stay. But the Court wanted to read what Circuit Court Judge Harry Pregerson had written in the fourth and last stay of execution, so Lungren was told to take Robert from the chamber.)

We were escorted back to Mosqueda's office to continue waiting. I shook uncontrollably for a long time, and cried openly. My escort suggested I needed medical attention, hinting I might have to leave. I forced back my tears and pulled myself together, although I could not stop trembling. Karen, the lawyer with us, picked up the heavy phone and dialed the office where lawyers who supported Harris had gathered. People there were crying. They did not know Robert had been spared from inside the chamber. They thought he was dead!

We resumed the grim vigil, cut off from the outside world. Just after 6 in the morning, I saw the witnesses from the victims' families being led past our window toward the chamber. Some were laughing. As honored guests, they had been playing video games, napping in the warden's home and eating specially prepared food. My heart stopped. Something was happening. Again, Karen called the same office and was told the stay of execution was still in place. But, as with the aborted execution attempt, they were the last to know.

Within fifteen seconds, the phone clattered to life, and Mendez told us the stay had been dissolved. (He did not tell us the Supreme Court had ordered all federal courts to enter no more stays of execution regardless of the issues.) We were going again.

Quickly we moved through the chill dawn air toward the chamber. Randy whispered in my ear, "Slow down." Near the entrance, Vernell Crittendon stood watching the procession move smoothly into the chamber. He pumped his upturned fist three times, the way football players do when their team has scored.

When they brought Robert in, he was grim-faced, tired and ashen. Beyond the horror of having stood at the brink of the abyss just two and a half hours before, he had been up for several days and nights. He was under horrific pressure. Again, he nodded to acquaintances. He did not smile. He faced to his right and said "I'm sorry" to the father of victim Michael Baker, the one family member he recognized from his endless rounds of television appearances. He craned his neck left once more and nodded quickly toward us. "It's all right," he reassured us. After about two minutes, he sniffed the air, then breathed deeply several times.

A Hideous Death

His head began to roll and his eyes closed, then opened again. His head dropped, then came up with an abrupt jerk, and rolled some more. It was grotesque and hideous, and I looked away. When I looked back, his head came up again and I covered my mouth. Randy was whimpering in pain next to me, and we clutched each other. The lawyer, sobbing audibly, put her arms around us and tried to comfort us. I could not stop shivering. Reverend Harris, Robert's second cousin and spiritual adviser, who had been with Robert in the holding cell almost until the moment they took him away, whispered, "He's ready. He was tired. It's all right. His punishment is over."

He writhed for seven minutes, his head falling on his chest, saliva drooling from his open mouth. He lifted his head again and again. Seven minutes. A lifetime. Nine more minutes passed with his head slumped on his chest. His heart, a survivor's heart, kept pumping for nine more minutes, while we held each other. Some of the witnesses laughed. I thought of the label "Laughing Killer," affixed to Robert by the media, and knew they would never describe these good people as laughing killers.

We were in the middle of something indescribably ugly. Not just the fact of the cold-blooded killing of a human being, and not even the fact that we happened to love him—but the ritual of it, the participation of us, the witnesses, the witnessing itself of this most private and personal act. It was nakedly barbaric. Nobody could say this had anything to do with justice, I thought. Yet this medieval torture chamber is what a large majority of my fellow Californians, including most in the room with me, believe in. The implications of this filled me with fear—fear for myself and for all of us, a fear I am ashamed to confess—while my friend was being strangled slowly to death in front of me.

Some witnesses began shuffling nervously. People looked at their watches. Then a guard stepped forward and announced that Robert Alton Harris, C.D.C. Prisoner B-66883, had expired in the gas chamber at 6:21 A.M., sixteen minutes after the cyanide had been gently lowered into the sulfuric acid. Sixteen minutes. He was a fighter to the end.

It was the moment Crittendon had been waiting for. He stepped into the middle of the quiet room, his Jheri-Kurls reflecting the eerie green light from the gas chamber where my friend lay dead, slumped forward against the straps in Chair B.

"Ladies and gentlemen. Please stay in your places until your escort comes for you. Follow your escort, as instructed. Thank you."

Our guard came and we followed him out. The eighteen media witnesses, who had stood against the wall opposite us scribbling on paper provided by the prison, preceded us out of the room. As they had been for weeks, they were desperate for a Harris family member to say something to them. "Is this a Harris? Is this a Harris?" a reporter standing just outside the door shouted, pointing at each of us as we emerged into the first light of morning over San Francisco Bay.

My god, it was a beautiful day.

A Test of Faith: Witnessing a Friend's Execution

William Vance Trollinger Jr.

William Vance Trollinger Jr. is an associate professor of history at the University of Dayton in Ohio. In the following article, Trollinger relates how his opposition to the death penalty and his Christian beliefs led him to begin corresponding with a death row inmate, Sam McDonald, in 1985. Trollinger explains how he and McDonald became friends over the years and how he reluctantly agreed to his friend's request to witness his execution in 1997. According to the author, only his faith in God helped him through the event, which he describes as a harrowing ordeal.

Just after midnight on Wednesday September 24, 1997, I watched as the state of Missouri put Samuel McDonald to death by lethal injection. I had never wanted to witness an execution, and I was devastated by what I saw. How did I come to be at the Potosi Correctional Institute on that night? It had to do with friendship, and with the unforeseen and frightening implications of taking even the smallest step forward in faith.

Since my late teens I have opposed the death penalty. I have had many reasons: Poor and minority defendants are executed in grossly disproportionate numbers. Innocent people are sometimes sentenced to death. There is no evidence that the death penalty reduces the rate of violent crime. The rest of the Western world has managed to function without executing criminals.

But the heart of my opposition grew out of my religious commitments. As a Christian, it seems to me that the death penalty violates the essence of Christ's teachings to choose mercy over revenge, to love our enemies and to forswear all violence.

For all of this, my opposition to capital punishment remained abstract. This was because, in the late 1960s, capital punishment almost disappeared from the American landscape. It seemed gone for good in 1972, when the U.S. Supreme Court (*Furman v. Georgia*) held that the death penalty is "arbitrary" and "capricious." But just four years later, the Court (*Gregg v. Georgia*) ruled that capital punishment

Reprinted from "My Friend's Execution," by William Vance Trollinger Jr., *Christian Century*, vol. 115, no. 31, November 11, 1998. Copyright ©1998 by Christian Century Foundation. Reprinted by permission of the November 11, 1998 issue of the *Christian Century*.

does not violate the Constitution as long as there are adequate due-process procedures. This ruling opened the door for states to resume their use of the death penalty. In the two decades since *Gregg v. Georgia*, 40 states have instituted it for certain types of murder.

Becoming Personally Involved

One of the states most eager to resume executions was Missouri. By the time I moved there in 1984, dozens of individuals had been sentenced to die. I was appalled. I wish I could say that I reacted by throwing myself (at least in some metaphorical sense) into the gears of Missouri's "killing machine." But the truth is that I acted on my moral outrage in a decidedly modest fashion. Following up on a notice in *The Other Side*, I contacted the Death Row Support Project for the name of a condemned prisoner with whom I could correspond. This is how I became acquainted with Samuel McDonald, or #CP-17, as he's known in the Missouri correctional system.

Sam grew up in a poor, churchgoing family in St. Louis. At 17 he enlisted in the army and ended up in Vietnam. He proved to be an efficient soldier, earning a raft of medals. But the experience traumatized him, particularly when, in the process of "sweeping" a village, he killed an infant and an elderly woman; he had nightmares about this incident for the rest of his life. Like a host of other Vietnam veterans, he returned to the States mentally and emotionally unhinged, and addicted to drugs.

On May 16, 1981, Sam, high on "T's and blues" (a heroin substitute), robbed and shot Robert Jordan, an off-duty police officer, as Jordan and his 11-year-old daughter were leaving a convenience store. A poor African-American drug addict shoots a police officer in front of the man's daughter: that could easily have been enough to ensure that Sam would be condemned to die. But Sam was also assigned an assistant public defender who got into shouting matches with the judge. Worse, the judge refused to allow testimony regarding Sam's Vietnam experiences and their impact on his mental and emotional health, even though there was evidence that Sam was suffering from a classic case of post-Vietnam stress syndrome. (This failure to order a psychiatric examination would be at the heart of Sam's appeals over the next 16 years.) It was no great surprise, therefore, that on February 22, 1982, Samuel McDonald was sentenced to death.

Three years later, in 1985, I sent Sam my first letter. We soon became regular correspondents. I also visited him twice at the penitentiary in Jefferson City where he was originally held.

When I took a teaching job in Pennsylvania, I was no longer able to visit. So Sam began calling. He would call every two or three weeks, and we would talk from 20 to 60 minutes. We spent a good amount of time making jokes and ribbing each other; in fact, if Sam called when we had friends visiting, they would often be stunned to learn that, given all of the laughter, I was talking with a man on death row. We also spent a lot of time talking about sports. Both of us were convinced that we had special insights into the game of football. We had an annual contest to see who could pick the most winners in the college bowl games, with the winner—usually Sam—receiving a "traveling crown" that Sam had made.

Of course, other conversations were much more serious. We talked about prison conditions, the status of his appeals and the Supreme Court. We talked about God, organized religion and the efficacy of prayer. We talked about our families. I commiserated with him, when his son—who was three when Sam went to prison, and whom Sam always referred to as "Little Sam"—was caught in the middle of a gang fight, and was shot and paralyzed. Sam commiserated with me when my mother died of cancer. In fact, he was probably more sensitive to my grief than anyone outside of my family; in the weeks after her death he would call just to see how I was coping.

Anguish and Virtue

The point is that Samuel McDonald and I became close friends. At the beginning of our correspondence I thought that I would be the one giving to Sam. But it turned out that I was receiving much more from him than I was giving. Sam also befriended my wife and daughters, sending them birthday and Christmas cards and occasionally talking with them on the phone.

As time went on, and my friendship with Sam deepened, I tried not to think about the fact that the state of Missouri was determined to end his life. But in the spring of 1997, reality hit. Sam had run out of opportunities for appeal when the Supreme Court did not stay his execution, and the governor of Missouri did not grant clemency. In other words, there was little reason for hope. Sam was given an execution date: September 24, 1997.

Sam handled these developments with remarkable grace, but I went into a severe emotional tailspin. I had begun writing to Sam out of my religious and political opposition to the death penalty. Now he was a close friend—and now he was going to be killed. But my personal anguish involved more than just Sam's impending death. I also agonized over what sort of friend I had been to Sam. In my mind, two shortcomings stood out. First, while Sam and I had frequently discussed religious faith, and while I had been forthright regarding my Christian convictions, I had not attempted and did not feel qualified to serve as Sam's "spiritual adviser," à la Sister Helen Préjean in *Dead Man Walking*. To compound my sense of failure, I could not bring myself to volunteer to serve as one of the witnesses to Sam's execution, even though I suspected that he wanted me to do just that.

During my time of distress, Father James Heft, chancellor at the University of Dayton (where I was now teaching), and Pastor Dorothy

Nickel Friesen of First Mennonite Church in Bluffton, Ohio (our home church), provided wise counsel. Jim suggested that I directly encourage Sam to take steps to "make things right" with God and with the family of the slain police officer—advice which I heeded in a letter that I wrote Sam that summer. Jim also reminded me that friendship was itself a Christian virtue. Dorothy pointed out that Christ requires not heroism—of which I was in short supply—but faithfulness. I did not volunteer to watch Sam be killed. But when he asked if I would serve as one of his "family and friend" witnesses, saying, "I don't want to die alone, and I need to see you there," I said yes.

Regrets and Resignation

On the morning of September 23, 1997, my wife, Gayle, and I drove to the Potosi Correctional Institute, southwest of St. Louis in the Ozark foothills. Sam had called to tell me that I would be allowed to visit him before the execution, so when we arrived at the isolated, fortress-like prison, Gayle dropped me off at the front gate. A guard took me to Sam. We descended endless flights of stairs into the depths of the prison. This is where the "death cell" is located, where all death-row inmates spend their last two days of life. The guard knocked on the door and I walked in.

There was Sam, rumpled and weary-looking, and heavier than when I had last seen him. He was in a tiny cage with a bed, a chair, a toilet and not much else. Instinctively I walked up to the wire fence and put my hand against it, greeting him in the same way I had a decade before. But before Sam could respond a voice behind me barked, "Get away from there!" Alarmed, I looked at Sam, and he pointed to the floor; a white line marked off a "no-man's-land" between the rest of humanity and Sam's cage. I backed up behind the line and sat down in one of two chairs bolted to the floor. To my right, another guard sat at a desk, clattering away on a very loud type-writer, presumably reporting on what was taking place in the cell. A video camera recorded everything that was going on. Sam McDonald's final 48 hours were without privacy, in part to ensure that he did not commit suicide and thus cheat the executioner.

At first, given these conditions, I struggled to make conversation with Sam. But in a few minutes we were talking freely. In some ways it was no different from our phone conversations. We talked about sports and our families; we talked about our friendship; we even had a few laughs. But then Sam talked about himself: he regretted how he had messed up his life, and expressed remorse for what he had done. I later learned from the *St. Louis Post-Dispatch* that he had made a public apology in an interview with a reporter. He assured me that he was prepared to die ("things on the other side have to be better than they have been over here") and to face God. For the first time in the 12 years that I had known Sam McDonald, he was resigned to his impending death.

At 5:58 my escort returned. I stood up; Sam and I said, "I love you" to each other. The door opened, and I left the death cell. Soon after I departed, Sam ate his last meal, which included steak, catfish and eggs. Soon after that the prison authorities began to prepare him for execution.

At 10:30 I was searched, then ushered into a cramped waiting room with Sam's five other witnesses: his son, cousin, attorney, minister and another pen pal. There were also a few guards who were quite affable and had the courtesy to stay relatively quiet—except when they proudly recounted how they had built a sturdy ramp that would permit Sam's son to be wheeled into position to view his father's execution. For the next 70 minutes we sat around the table and talked about Sam. From his cousin and minister I learned about his childhood and his family. From his attorney I learned that Sam had good reason to have been optimistic about his appeals, given that he was a much-decorated veteran who had been denied the opportunity to present an adequate defense. With only a slight change in the circumstances of his trial and appeals, with only one small break somewhere in the process, Samuel McDonald might have spent a good deal of time, perhaps even the remainder of his life, in prison. He would not have been executed.

Suddenly the phone rang, and one of the guards answered it. He told us that the time had come, then warned us that "there will be no standing, crying out or knocking on the window," and marched us to our destination. The execution chamber was conveniently situated near the death cell, thus allowing for an efficient execution that did not interfere with "normal" prison life.

Renewed Convictions

In Missouri there are three observation booths: one for the family of the crime victim, one for the state witnesses and one for family and friends of the condemned. The six of us were ushered into the latter, a tiny room that reminded me of a poorly appointed viewing box at a sports stadium. There was seating room for six witnesses in our booth, three in front and three in back. Squeezing into the booth with us were four guards, who flanked us on all sides, and who apparently were there to ensure that there would be no inappropriate emotional outbursts on our part.

I ended up in the front row, just inches from the viewing window; the blinds were closed, but through a crack I could see movement, and Sam's jaw and mouth. As I sat in that cramped booth, waiting and looking at the tiny fragment of my friend, I was overwhelmed by dread. As a middle-class, middle-aged white man who grew up in suburbia and has lived a secure and privileged life, I had never seen anyone die, much less be killed. Now I had a front-row seat. I would see Sam McDonald poisoned with a lethal combination of sodium pentothal, which would render him unconscious, and pancuronium bromide and potassium bromide, which would shut down his breathing and his heart.

Just after midnight the guards raised the blinds. There, in a dazzling white room, lay Sam. He was on a gurney with a white sheet up to his neck; from my vantage point, I could not see that he was strapped down, and that he was hooked up to a mechanical apparatus. Directly across from us was the booth containing the state witnesses (including journalist Christopher Hitchens, who wrote about his experience in *Vanity Fair*). I could not see the booth with the family of the murdered police officer.

Sam had obviously been briefed as to where his family and friends would be located, because he looked only at us. He was speaking rapidly, but we could not hear anything. I repeatedly mouthed "I love you" to him; others flashed the peace sign, or put their hands up in prayer. Behind me I could hear faint crying. Then, after a minute or two, the deadly drugs kicked in. Sam briefly shuddered. His eyes fluttered. And then he was still.

For the next few minutes we sat looking at him. Then the guards shut the blinds and ushered us out of the observation booth and back into the waiting room. While we gathered our coats and belongings someone in our group suggested that Sam's minister lead us in prayer. But before he could respond, one of the guards hastily intervened: "We will have none of that in here." I wish now that I had defied this edict and dropped to my knees on the concrete floor; but instead, numbed by the horror I had just witnessed, I followed the escort out of the room, through the courtyard and beyond the prison walls.

Leaving Potosi did not mean that I could escape what I had seen. For 48 hours after the execution I felt an extreme compulsion to shower and shower and shower again. Eventually I realized that I felt filthy because I had observed an obscenity. Never in my life have I been so aware of the reality of evil as I was in that observation booth, watching the deliberate, methodical and antiseptic killing of Samuel McDonald, a killing done by the state of Missouri in the name of its citizens. For a long time I have known, intellectually, that capital punishment is wrong. Now I feel it—it's visceral.

I also learned something about what it means to follow Christ. I began writing letters to Samuel McDonald because I thought it was the easiest and safest way I could follow through on my convictions. Moreover, when it became clear that the state of Missouri was going to have its way, I desperately hoped that Sam would not ask me to witness his execution. Yet my tiny step taken in faith led me into deep and cold waters, where the grace of God sufficed to keep me from drowning, but not from feeling enormous pain, anger and despair.

Organizations to Contact

The editors have compiled the following list of organizations concerned with the issues presented in this book. The descriptions are derived from materials provided by the organizations. All have publications or information available for interested readers. The list was compiled on the date of publication of the present volume; the information provided here may change. Be aware that many organizations take several weeks or longer to respond to inquiries, so allow as much time as possible.

American Civil Liberties Union (ACLU)
Capital Punishment Project
122 Maryland Ave. NE, Washington, DC 20002
(202) 675-2321

The ACLU's Capital Punishment Project is dedicated to abolishing the death penalty. The ACLU believes that capital punishment violates the Constitution's ban on cruel and unusual punishment as well as the requirements of due process and equal protection under the law. It publishes and distributes numerous books and pamphlets, including *The Case Against the Death Penalty* and *Frequently Asked Questions Concerning the Writ of Habeas Corpus and the Death Penalty.*

Amnesty International USA
Program to Abolish the Death Penalty
322 Eighth Ave., 10th Floor, New York, NY 10001
(212) 633-4280
e-mail: mundies@aiusa.org • website: www.amnesty-usa.org/abolish/

Amnesty International's Program to Abolish the Death Penalty works to eliminate capital punishment worldwide. The program seeks to progressively decrease the use of the death penalty and to increase the number of U.S. states and nations that have removed the death penalty from their legal codes. It publishes the reports *The Death Penalty: List of Abolitionist and Retentionist Countries* and *Facts and Figures on the Death Penalty* several times a year.

Catholics Against Capital Punishment (CACP)
PO Box 3125, Arlington, VA 22203-8125
phone and fax: (301) 652-1125
e-mail: cacp@bellatlantic.net • website: www2.dcci.com/ltlflwr/CACP.html

Catholics Against Capital Punishment is a national advocacy organization that works to abolish the death penalty in the United States. CACP was founded in 1992 to promote greater awareness of Catholic Church teachings that characterize capital punishment as inappropriate and unacceptable in today's world. It publishes *CACP News Notes* four to six times a year.

Death Penalty Information Center (DPIC)
1320 18th St. NW, 5th Floor, Washington, DC 20036
(202) 293-6970 • fax: (202) 822-4787
e-mail: dpic@essential.org • website: www.essential.org/dpic

DPIC provides the media and the public with analysis and information on issues concerning capital punishment. The center opposes capital punishment, believing that it is discriminatory, excessively costly, and may result in the execution of innocent persons. It publishes numerous reports, such as *Millions*

Misspent: What Politicians Don't Say About the High Costs of the Death Penalty, Innocence and the Death Penalty: Assessing the Danger of Mistaken Executions, and *With Justice for Few: The Growing Crisis in Death Penalty Representation.*

The Friends Committee to Abolish the Death Penalty (FCADP)
3721 Midvale Ave., Philadelphia, PA 19129
(215) 951-0330 • fax: (215) 951-0342
e-mail:fcadp@aol.com • website: www.quaker.org/fcadp/

The Friends Committee to Abolish the Death Penalty is a national Quaker organization that was established in 1993. FCADP publishes a quarterly newsletter, the *Quaker Abolitionist.*

Justice Fellowship
PO Box 16069, Washington, DC 20041-6069
(703) 904-7312 • fax: (703) 478-9679
website: www.justicefellowship.org

The Justice Fellowship is a national criminal justice reform organization that advocates victims' rights, alternatives to prison, and community involvement in the criminal justice system. It aims to make the criminal justice system more consistent with biblical teachings on justice. It does not take a position on the death penalty, but it publishes the pamphlet *Capital Punishment: A Call to Dialogue.*

Justice Now
PO Box 62132, North Charleston, SC 29419-2132

Justice Now supports the death penalty as a solution to the problems of crime and overcrowded prisons in the United States. It maintains information resources, which it makes available to the public, consisting of books, pamphlets, periodicals, newspaper clippings, and bibliographies on the subjects of serial killers, death row prisoners, executions, prisons, and the courts.

Lamp of Hope Project
13931 N. Central Expressway, Suite 246, Dallas, TX 75243-1013
(615) 791-6496

The Lamp of Hope Project was established and is primarily run by Texas death row inmates. It works to address victims' rights and legal issues, the effects of poverty on crime, and the concerns of children and other family members of incarcerated individuals, especially those on death row. The group publishes the periodic *Texas Death Row Journal.*

Lincoln Institute for Research and Education
1001 Connecticut Ave. NW, Suite 1135, Washington, DC 20036
(202) 223-5112

The institute is a conservative think tank that studies public policy issues affecting the lives of black Americans, including the issue of capital punishment, which it favors. It publishes the quarterly *Lincoln Review.*

NAACP Legal Defense and Education Fund
99 Hudson St., Suite 1600, New York, NY 10013-2897
(212) 219-1900

Founded by the National Association for the Advancement of Colored People (NAACP), the fund opposes the death penalty and works to end discrimination in the justice system. It compiles and reports statistics on the death penalty and publishes legal material, fact sheets, and reports.

National Criminal Justice Reference Service (NCJRS)
U.S. Department of Justice
PO Box 6000, Rockville, MD 20850-6000
(800) 851-3420 • fax: (301) 519-5212
e-mail: askncjrs@ncjrs.org • website: www.ncjrs.org

NCJRS is an international clearinghouse that provides information and research about criminal justice. It works in conjunction with the National Institute of Justice and the Office of Juvenile Justice. NCJRS publishes various reports and journals pertaining to the criminal justice system.

National Legal Aid and Defender Association (NLADA)
1625 K St. NW, 8th Floor, Washington, DC 20006
(201) 452-0620
e-mail: info@nlada.org • website: www.nlada.org

NLADA provides technical assistance to and acts as an information clearing-house for organizations that provide legal aid and services to the poor. It advocates high-quality legal services for the indigent. The association publishes material to assist legal-services organizations and distributes reports by death penalty opponents.

BIBLIOGRAPHY

Books

James R. Acker, Robert M. Bohm, and Charles S. Lanier, eds.	*America's Experiment with Capital Punishment: Reflections on the Past, Present, and Future of the Ultimate Penal Sanction.* Durham, NC: Carolina Academic Press, 1998.
Amnesty International	*Fatal Flaws: Innocence and the Death Penalty in the USA.* New York: Amnesty International USA, 1998.
Hugo Adam Bedau	*The Case Against the Death Penalty.* Washington, DC: American Civil Liberties Union, 1997.
John D. Bessler	*Death in the Dark: Midnight Executions in America.* Boston: Northeastern University Press, 1997.
Alan I. Bigel	*Justices William J. Brennan Jr. and Thurgood Marshall on Capital Punishment: Its Constitutionality, Morality, Deterrent Effect, and Interpretation by the Court.* Lanham, MD: University Press of America, 1997.
Donald A. Cabana	*Death at Midnight: The Confession of an Executioner.* Boston: Northeastern University Press, 1996.
Mark Costanzo	*Just Revenge: Costs and Consequences of the Death Penalty.* New York: St. Martin's Press, 1997.
Shirley Dicks, ed.	*Young Blood: Juvenile Justice and the Death Penalty.* Amherst, NY: Prometheus Books, 1995.
Richard J. Evans	*Rituals of Retribution: Capital Punishment in Germany, 1600–1987.* New York: Oxford University Press, 1996.
L. Kay Gillespie	*Dancehall Ladies: The Crimes and Executions of America's Condemned Women.* Lanham, MD: University Press of America, 1997.
Herbert H. Haines	*Against Capital Punishment: The Anti-Death Penalty Movement in America, 1972–1994.* New York: Oxford University Press, 1999.
Robert L. Hale	*A Review of Juvenile Executions in America.* Lewiston, NY: Edwin Mellen Press, 1997.
Roger G. Hood	*The Death Penalty: A World-wide Perspective.* New York: Oxford University Press, 1996.
Robert Johnson	*Death Work: A Study of the Modern Execution Process.* Belmont, CA: Wadsworth, 1998.
Barry Latzer	*Death Penalty Cases.* Boston: Butterworth-Heinemann, 1998.
David Lester	*The Death Penalty: Issues and Answers.* Springfield, IL: Charles C. Thomas, 1998.
Robert Emmet Long, ed.	*Criminal Sentencing.* New York: H.W. Wilson, 1995.

Desmond Manderson, ed.	*Courting Death: The Law of Mortality.* Sterling, VA: Pluto Press, 1999.
Michael A. Mello	*Dead Wrong: A Death Row Lawyer Speaks Out Against Capital Punishment.* Madison: University of Wisconsin Press, 1997.
Jeffrie G. Murphy, ed.	*Punishment and Rehabilitation.* Belmont, CA: Wadsworth, 1995.
Kathleen A. O'Shea	*Women and the Death Penalty in the United States, 1900–1998.* Westport, CT: Praeger, 1999.
Austin Sarat, ed.	*The Killing State: Capital Punishment in Law, Politics, and Culture.* New York: Oxford University Press, 1999.
Glen H. Stassen, ed.	*Capital Punishment: A Reader.* Cleveland: Pilgrim Press, 1998.
Bryan Vila and Cynthia Morris, eds.	*Capital Punishment in the United States: A Documentary History.* Westport, CT: Greenwood Press, 1997.

Periodicals

American Bar Association	"The Death Penalty: A Scholarly Forum," *Focus on Law Studies,* Spring 1997. Available from the American Bar Association, 750 N. Lake Shore Dr., Chicago, IL 60611.
Walter Berns and Joseph Bessette	"Why the Death Penalty Is Fair," *Wall Street Journal,* January 9, 1998.
Sharon Brownlee, Dan McGraw, and Jason Vest	"The Place for Vengeance," *U.S. News & World Report,* June 16, 1997.
David Cole	"Courting Capital Punishment," *Nation,* February 26, 1996.
Don Corrigan	"Viewing Executions: Does the Public Have the Right to See?" *St. Louis Journalism Review,* March 1999.
Stuart A. Creque	"Killing with Kindness," *National Review,* September 11, 1995.
John J. DiIulio Jr.	"Abolish the Death Penalty, Officially," *Wall Street Journal,* December 15, 1997.
Suzanne Donovan	"Shadow Figures: A Portrait of Life on Death Row," *Mother Jones,* July 29, 1997.
Robert F. Drinan	"Catholic Politicians and the Death Penalty," *America,* May 1, 1999.
Jean Bethke Elshtain	"Sacrilege," *New Republic,* June 16, 1997.
Ted Gest	"A House Without a Blueprint: After 20 Years the Death Penalty Is Still Being Meted Out Unevenly," *U.S. News & World Report,* July 8, 1996.
Steven Hawkins	"Death at Midnight . . . Hope at Sunrise," *Corrections Today,* August 1996.
Christopher Hitchens	"Scenes from an Execution," *Vanity Fair,* January 1998.
David A. Kaplan	"Life and Death Decisions," *Newsweek,* June 16, 1997.

John Kavanaugh   "Killing Persons, Killing Ethics," *America*, July 19, 1997.

Anthony Lewis   "Emotion, Not Reason," *New York Times*, January 2, 1998.

Peter Linebaugh   "The Farce of the Death Penalty," *Nation*, August 14–21, 1995.

Kelly McMurry   "Wearing the Toughness Badge: States Hurry to Carry Out Executions," *Trial*, March 1996.

Caroline Moorehead   "Tinkering with Death," *World Press Review*, July 1995.

Richard John Neuhaus "A Position Not, or Not Yet, Mandated," *First Things*, April 1998. Available from 156 Fifth Ave., Suite 400, New York, NY 10010.

Eric Pooley   "Death or Life?" *Time*, June 16, 1997.

Helen Préjean   "There's No Living with the Death Penalty," *Ms.*, May/June 1996.

INDEX